ISBN: 1460916875
ISBN-13: 9781460916872

TABLE OF CONTENTS

INTRODUCTION

Where does one begin telling a tale of such proportion it is almost impossible for the mind to comprehend? This is a tale about life in prison, jail, correctional detention center, or whatever term best fits being incarcerated. It really doesn't matter because all of them are *hell* on earth.

This book was not written to present my personal story or account why I was arrested—it is about living—surviving—while being incarcerated. Other than those revolving door inmates staying for a day, weekend, or even a week, the amount of time is really unimportant, as being incarcerated quickly becomes a life style all of its own. That is not to say a person can't get injured or even killed within minutes of being thrown into such a place; it is just that they don't have the time to become acclimated, or to get over the initial shock of what is happening to them. They don't have the time to try to learn how life in prison works.

I already know one thing; I will upset inmates by using the words, "jail," "prison," and "correctional detention facility" interchangeably. Also, the way I use "probation" and "parole" interchangeably. Deal with it! I know how my doing this with words would set off many inmates while I was in there, but it goes to show how ignorant people are about our penal system.

So, if I'm not going to tell my story about my own personal case, then what is this book about? I am hoping to keep this book an honest account of what it is like to be imprisoned, talking mostly about the common daily events and the way a prisoner lives and survives with them, life events like eating, sleeping, living in a cell, the dining and common area, hygiene, holidays, watching TV, entertainment (or lack of), inmates, guards, lawyers, judges, court, the system, healthcare providers (nurses), shake downs, visitation, talking on the PAY TEL phone system, fights. It also addresses the mental aspects of being incarcerated, generalities about inmates, ice treats, not seeing the sun or sky or trees or grass, and most importantly, *time*. This was all new to my wife (on the outside) and me at our ages; it was a life event we definitely could have done without.

There is some information about my account of events and my case. This is my personal perception as to what all took place. There are aspects about myself that are very relevant to writing my perspective. This was my first incarceration. I turned 52 years old while in jail. I suffered in jail while birthdays, holidays, world events, work, church, and on and on happened without me. The worst thing was missing my wife's birthday.

The worst and most important aspect of being in jail does is the terrible impact on the lives of loved ones, friends, fellow workers, and too many other people to mention. I want to especially express my most sincere apology and love to my wife for staying with me through this hell; she stayed strong and helped us to recover. Yes—to recover. I will cover this in more detail, but what most movies and stories don't depict is there is a long and difficult recovery period after being released. Thank you, you dear! She had the strength of the Lord with her, and He is the reason we were able to survive this ordeal. God was there to help us through each and every day—we know that for sure.

IN THE BEGINNING

Like the old cliché goes, the best place to start is in the beginning. I will begin with my arrival and the in-processing desk of the correctional detention center where I resided. This is not about the events leading up to my being placed into jail or my case. Again—this is about living in jail.

I was totally stunned and dazed when I first arrived. Not because I was being in- processed, but from the brutal beating I received and being tazered by the police earlier (naturally no record of any of that occurring). The officer that "greeted" me at the counter was a very large, black, with a shaved head. A very intimidating individual with a nasty disposition, to say the least. I politely answered his questions, still cuffed and shackled. When he informed me I was going to be fingerprinted, I asked him when I was going to be read my rights. He said this was not the place that was done. Without a fuss I merely refused to be fingerprinted. Big mistake! I was placed in a cell about 8 feet by 6 feet, with a 2 foot-by-3 foot concrete slab to sit or lie on. There was no blanket to keep warm. I hardly any clothes on. It was freezing. After 4 hours of this he again informed me that I was to be fingerprinted. This time I asked to speak to an attorney. Another big mistake! Four more hours in that cell, that I later learned was called the "hole." There are hell hole cells all over the facility. Eight hours of enduring the hole was enough. I let them fingerprint me and would have done most anything they wanted at that point. I also learned later that my actions would come back to haunt me. I was labeled a "troublemaker" in my folder, and my medical portion of the documents was never completed. I have been on blood pressure medicine for 30 years. This "label" caused me a great amount of trouble to get any type of blood-pressure medicine.

Fingerprints now taken and in-processing completed, I was taken to be stripped and showered. The guard checked in my personal items—a tee shirt, flannel pants, and slippers. I was ready for bed at home when all this began. He handed me my dark-blue jump suit, "Bob Barker" flip flops for shoes, a paper-thin sheet that was 5 feet by 5 feet, a horse-hair, old GI blanket that was 5 feet x 5 feet, and a 16-ounce plastic cup—this cup would become critical. Inmates are only issued one plastic cup for as long as they stay. If it cracked or you lost your cup you had to steal or trade for a new cup. I had no underwear.

I was all in-processed, prison dressed, and ready to begin a whole new life. The guard took me to the door and pointed down the hall, telling me to go to E POD. Like I know what a pod is and what E stands for. Keep in mind, I am still stunned, in pain, and in total shock. I walked down what appeared to be a sterile, white, CMU-block hallway, with numerous doors, all with strange labels, and a tile floor—grey tiles on each side and white tiles down the middle. I finally found some doors with different titles. The E on the label of a door finally appeared. This door had a window. Peering through the window, I could see people inside. Some were wearing the same dark-blue jump suit. I would later learn jumps suits are different colors, as the colors indicated the degree of security to the guards. I knocked on the door, and nothing. It was as thick and hard as the CMU brick walls, but I continued to knock. Nothing! Finally, I heard a voice yell, "Push the button, stupid!" This voice came from a control room. One at each end of the hallway. These rooms were where the guards keep an eye on what is going on in the halls—command and control points or in military lingo—C2. The windows to these control points were dark tinted, but one learned how to see in after being incarcerated a while. These were where two guards who watched monitors to various areas of their responsibility, and watched inmates walking in the halls. I pushed the button, and the door finally opened. I stepped into a controlled, glassed area between the hallway and the place that would become my new home—E POD. A guard standing inside the big room pushed a button to let me in.

I was sick and sore as a dog for the first few weeks being in prison. The arresting police had put a hurting on me. The worst part about the pain was I hurt in so many places lying down was difficult and painful. The back of my head had a nice-sized lump. Both my eyes were blackened, and one was really puffy. I had a place in the middle of my back that just ached all day long. This is where the police placed the tazer. Also two fingers on my left hand were broken, and they still hurt when I made a fist. I already had three broken ribs on the left side of my chest. They hurt when I just breathed. Forget lying on the side with my broken ribs on the metal bunk or the concrete floor. My blood pressure was sky high, and I'd get dizzy just standing or sitting. Walking made me ill. I still limped from the pain in my knee where the officers pounded me with flashlights. You could see the imprint of a hand bruise on my right arm where the officers picked me up and slung me around while my hands were cuffed behind me. They laughed and took great pleasure in inflicting pain on me.

As if all that wasn't bad enough, I know my mind and body were suffering from being tazered. Mostly at night time when I'd get still, I'd have strange jolts shoot through the joints of my body and my head. My vision still became blurred and seemed to get worse with each day. The jolts occurred in one joint location at a time, but continuously through my body at night when I'd try to get my body relaxed. These jolts would be so violent my body would literally jump, like a body does when jolted with an electric defibrillator used when paramedics think your heart has stopped. These jolts would continually go off inside my head, my shoulders, and the organs in my body, my knees, ankles, and feet. Now all my joints ached. I seldom slept through the night for the pain in the knuckles of my hand, my shoulders, hips, and knees. I'm sure the jolts throughout my body and pain in my major joints were a result from being tazered. I thought at the time while the arresting police were abusing me severely, that they were using brass knuckle on me. The brass knuckles turned out to be tazers. I have since learned the brass-knuckle-shaped tazers are the best selling and most powerful tazers on the market. The police never admitted to using a tazer on me. For that matter there is no court record I was even arrested. All the wounds were self inflicted—I guess.

DAILY SCHEDULE

Before I get too far ahead of myself let me describe the daily schedule or routines. The day started at 6 a.m. with the waking of the trustees. Trustees were usually long-term prisoners selected primarily for good behavior and the ability to take control of the other inmates residing in the correctional detention facility. Size was not necessarily a prerequisite. We had one very small older trustee, but he had the respect of most of the inmates. Size was definitely an asset, though, since trustees were often confronted by the other inmates for a number of reasons. Again, I will talk more about the role of trustees later. The trustees got up and were let out of their cells to get the place ready for a new day. By 6:15 a.m. the guards started waking the 80 inmates. Usually the yell of "Chow Call!" was enough, but there were always the slow walkers. Some guards took care of this problem by opening doors for a few minutes, and if an inmate was not out of his cell and headed for the chow line then his cell door would be locked, and no breakfast. Breakfast was the start of each day at about 6:30 a.m.

Meal times were when racial divides became prevalent. The small round tables sat four inmates. Hispanics most always congregated together. Most of the blacks and whites sat segregated from each other. There were some inmates who didn't care who they sat with. They just wanted to eat in peace. Then there were friendships that broke the racial divide. There was not one oriental or Middle Eastern individual in the POD.

As inmates finished breakfast, they took the food trays back up, and most began to hunt down cleaning supplies. Keeping one's cell clean was mostly a health concern for most inmates, but it was also something to pass the time. It was also the time for the chemical druggies to try to cop a buzz from the cleaning materials. Here are some details about cleaning the cells and cleaning supplies. Cleaning the cells began right after breakfast. Cleaning the cell doesn't take long. The trustees are cleaning the dining area while inmates are running around like chickens with their heads cut off to get a hold of the cleaning materials to do their cells. Cleaning tables after meals is one of the trustee's chores, but they receive benefits for doing extra duties. There isn't much of anything an inmate does unless there is something in it for them—unless it is some type of punishment.

Each day different activities are scheduled for different times. For now I will tell about the regular, routine things that take place during a day. So now breakfast and cleaning one's cell is done. It is about 8 a.m. and the TVs are put on. It is basically free time. I would usually go back to the bunk and try to get a little more sleep. It seemed like the only sleep I got was the time just before wake-up call. The entire time I was in jail I seldom got more than an hour or two of sleep most nights. My high blood pressure didn't allow me to keep any sort of a regular routine. In the beginning I prayed I would just sleep this nightmare away. No such luck! Sleep for most inmates came when you were so tired you'd pass out. The nightmares while actually sleeping were the worst. Hell on earth or being in prison cannot compare to the nightmares. They are so bad my mind won't let me remember them—and I don't want to!

The nurses came for the morning "Pill Call" usually shortly after breakfast. I missed my pills a few times from going back to the bunk to take a nap. Some guards were nice enough to call down to the nurses' station and send me to get the pills I missed, but oftentimes I was just out of luck until the next "Pill Call" that evening, 12 hours later. I was a mess when I didn't get my meds as that meant I was to go for at least 12 hours between pill calls. Hours without my blood pressure medicine. No fun! Deadly!

Next on the schedule for the day was lunch from about 11 to 11:30 a.m. Lunch lock-down starts about 10:00 a.m. before the food is served. Lock-down is when the inmates go to their cells. The cells were then locked down until the guards opened the doors. This was time for the trustees to get chairs and tables ready for the meal. Plus, it offered some rest time for the guards from the stress that had been taking place that morning. I'll admit being a guard has to be about as stressful a job as one can imagine. There are grumpy inmates at all different hours of the day, but most irritability was during the morning. The place is still noisy as hell, but not as noisy as later in the afternoon and evening times. Breakfast and lunch usually went without incidents, as inmates were grumpy, but their energy hadn't really kicked in for the day.

The same routine was repeated at about 2:30 p.m. as inmates were locked down for dinner to be served between 3 and 3:30 p.m. This was way too early for dinner, but who said prison was made to cater to the inmates? Still—15 hours between meals is a bit much. This amount of time between meals generally created most of the violence. Inmates were already getting hungry just before lock-down for the night at 10 p.m.

Most of the violence was shouting and pushing, but there was the occasional fight between 2 inmates. There were only a few times I witnessed fights of more than 2 inmates. Not many wanted to go to solitary confinement. Depending on how serious the incident, an inmate could spend anywhere from a few days, to 90 days, or up to 3 years for fighting. This included the inmate in self defense if he struck back. Crazy!

Now all the inmates were in their cells and locked down for the night at 10 p.m. This was letter-writing time, or quiet time before lights out at 11 p.m. This is when all hell would break out. There were the door kickers and hitters. There were the screamers and criers. All this crap would go on into the wee hours of the night. The night-time guards, 6 p.m. to 6 a.m. would tolerate most anything except violence in the cells. What were they suppose to do—send every inmate to solitary confinement? Sometimes they would put an inmate on lock-down for 4 to 8 hours the next day, but that punishment was up to the day-shift guards as to whether they wanted to deal with more noise. Usually not, and the inmates knew this. So that is the general schedule of a day and night in prison.

HOME—E POD

I don't remember much about the first few days permanently in my new place of residence—E POD. All I can figure is "POD" stands for Place of Detention, and the E is the identifier of the POD in which an inmate resides. There were two guards permanently assigned to a POD 24/7. They worked 12-hour shifts and seldom left the POD. Most teams of guards consisted of a male and a female. They were police officers, and this was their job. Upon entering, I was at what was called "the guards' console." This is where the guards spend most of their time. They have electronic controls for the opening and closing of all the cell doors. They have an intercom system to each cell, but seldom use it except at night so they don't wake other inmates. Upon entering I was hand-patted down for any possible contraband on my person, and the items I was provided were also searched. The guard then pointed for me to go to my cell "10". Still dazed and in pain I walked to the cell without noticing the other inmates or my surroundings.

Upon my entering there was a young man lying in the top bunk. Cells were approximately 12 feet by 10 feet, with a normal-sized metal door. The door has a double-pane glass window that is about 3 foot by 18 inches. The window serves two purposes. One is for the inmate to look out. The second is for the guards to look in. There are two stacked metal bunk beds—racks. The guard or trustee provided me with a 6-foot-by-3-foot plastic mattress that was about 2 inches thick. The mattress felt very thin. There was a small hole at each end of the pad to release the air inside. This must be where the fairy tale "The Princess and the Pea" came from, since you can feel even the smallest particle on or under the mattress. Also, any creases in the mattress, blanket, or clothing became painful and sometimes created sores. There was a slight lump at one end of the mattress that is considered the pillow. Behind the bunks were a stainless steel toilet and sink. Above the sink was a small, unbreakable mirror—it actually distorted one's face enough to scare a person. Next to that was a small metal desk with a small, round, pull-out metal seat. A 3-foot-by-twofoot plastic Tupperware box was provided for each inmate. Both boxes were stored under the bottom bunk. Beds were to be made each day. How bunks were to be made was anyone's guess; they just had to be made in some manner.

Leaving one's cell you entered into what was called the common area. 80 inmates were in a POD. All ate in the common area. It was carpeted: filthy dirty, but carpeted. The common area consisted of about 20 round 3-foot tables and 80 plastic garden chairs. Inmates played cards, watched TV, sat in chairs, and ate sitting in the same chairs. There were 8 PAY TEL phones (most didn't work, and those that did barely worked). Other than writing letters these crappy rip-off of phones were the only connection to the outside world. There was one toilet in the common area for 80 men to share. It had one toilet and sink, usually no toilet paper, and never any soap or towels for washing one's hands after going to the bathroom. There were two other rooms. One was a small, multipurpose room, and the other, what used to be the smoke area, was now a very small, concrete, single-goal basketball area. The facility was now smoke free. The 40 cells were split into 20 cells upstairs and 20 cells downstairs.

There were occasions when inmates were allowed to leave the POD and venture into the hallway. The best reason was to go to visitation. The second-best reason was going to the commissary to buy snacks or odds and ends if there was money in your prison account. There was going to the nurses' station, and I use that term "nurse" very loosely. One got to go see one's attorney, went to court, or guards mistakenly sent you somewhere. Hell—they release inmates by mistake for a variety of mistakes: paperwork, being tired, sending the wrong person called, and misspelling of names are a few examples. Most everything in the place is painted white, and it all stinks. Doors, carpet, console, and a few other things are of some drab color. There are no windows to the outside, and no one went outside for any reason while in this facility. I know TV shows have inmates outside at different facilities across the US, but nobody staying at this place ever saw the outside except when released. That should give somewhat of picture of what a POD looks like and some sense of what living in the place is like.

THE CELL

I just described what a cell looks like—now let me talk more about what it is like to live in a cell. An inmate did not have any say as to who they would share a cell with. Like most anything else, there were ways around this, but in general there was no say. An inmate might get moved for a variety of reasons; the most prevalent is for fighting. That usually resulted in a permanent move to solitary confinement. Racism was probably the primary reason for major arguments and fights. This was the easiest way one could fake to get moved to a friend's cell—but that got complicated as the friend had to be the only inmate in that cell at the time. A cell mate with bad hygiene was another reason to be allowed to move to another cell. Some inmates never showered or brushed their teeth. Bad breath stunk the entire place up. Even with all the cleaning rules in place prisons are very unsanitary.

Clutter also became a major problem, as there should be little to none. The best analogy I can use for describing this is a true story that I once read in a science magazine. A company put a building out in the middle of a desert to do some type of research. They built a small oasis and plants around it. It wasn't long before different varieties of plants began sprouting up out of the ground. Fish began to appear in the small pond. Other creatures, such as turtles, and small rodents also showed up. Birds were bringing in the animals and vegetation in their bills. The point is that you can take a tiny cell, with little to nothing being allowed to get into it, yet in a short period of time it can become cluttered with garbage. Then horrible smells mount up.

JAIL

Taking a crap while your roommate is stuck in the cell to endure the smell was also a major cause for disturbances. This could be unbearable sometimes. Yes—it is an act of nature, but fights broke out over this. Farts, bad breath, and taking a dump were the cause of some fights. Most inmates tried to use the one common area toilet if possible, to not piss off their cell mates. You don't take too long in that common-area bathroom or you will have a bunch of inmates pissed off at you. The common-area toilet is located right where the food trays are wheeled in and served. Adds to the aroma!

I spent a good part of my spare time writing my wife letters— almost every day and night. The metal chair attached to the desk became unbearable to sit on. I'd do everything imaginable to try to cushion it. I would fold the small shower towel to sit on. I would fold the sheet to sit on. I would fold the blanket to sit on. Sometimes I would sit on all of them. It hurt my back something terrible to sit at the desk. Why not go out in the common area and sit at those tables and chairs? That was taboo. I learned many of the inmates didn't know how to read or write, so it was like flaunting your educational skills. Also, many didn't have any family or friends to write to. Writing out in the common area would also attract inmates to come over and pester you, wanting you to write for them, and that caused trouble, so it wasn't worth it to be comfortable sitting and writing. I learned how to write sitting on my bunk. Thank goodness most of the time I had a bottom bunk. Just trying to sleep on the metal bunk with 3 broken ribs was awful. I couldn't even get an aspirin for the pain. I couldn't climb to a top bunk, and we'll talk later about the short period I was put on a top bunk and ended up sleeping on the concrete floor.

Let me tell you about a 6-foot-tall, 200-pound man trying to sleep and stay warm with a 5-foot-by-5-foot horsehair blanket. You can't! Now the jump suit we wore 24/7 (swapped out twice a week) did little to keep you warm during the day, and the little blanket did less to keep you warm at night. I tried everything. Wrapping the sheet around my feet and legs and wrapping the blanket around my upper body. I felt like a damn mummy. I tried putting the blanket in a diamond shape, but nothing worked. Why was it so cold throughout the facility? It was to keep the place sterile and germ free. Nothing worse than getting sick while incarcerated, and I did. I talked about being able to feel the smallest particle under the mattress, which was so thin, and the metal bunk or concrete floor being so hard. Wrinkles in the jump suit, the sheet, or blanket would become painful while trying to get to sleep. Then there was the constant noise all night long.

I said no pillows were issued. The little lump of a pillow in the mattress did nothing to elevate one's head. Inmates had to really improvise here. Inmates didn't share information with each other. For example, nothing was necessarily what it seemed to be. My Bob Barker flip flops became my pillow. No one shared this idea with me; I just figured that you put one flip flop inside the other and put them under the mattress, and Voila! You have a pillow. Well, at least your head is elevated some.

Days later when I was finally able to call my wife, tell her where I was, and what was going on, she was then able to put a little money in my prison account so I could go to the commissary. I bought 2 tee shirts, 2 boxer shorts, 2 pairs of white socks, and a few snacks. All items sold at outrageous prices. Some were free samples, and it stated right on the package, "Not to be sold." The best rip-off was that Chap Stick came with a sample Blistex tube. They took the sample off and sold it separately. The same bags of chips were 10 cents more than what they cost in the guard's vending machine. The Bob Barker products said, "Not for sale," but they sold them. Toothbrush, toothpaste, soap, shampoo, and all were labeled not to be sold. The prices were outrageous.

Back to the pillow. I would now use a tee shirt folded up as my pillow. The socks would keep my feet and legs warm. Sometimes I would put socks over my hands and arms to keep them warm. How I survived before getting these clothes only God knows.

There was screaming and howling all night long. Jerks would kick and bang on the doors, walls, and scream into the vents. The duct system basically connected the upper cell and cell below it. Noises were amplified through the vents. With the constant turnover of inmates one might have a period where noises and talking through vents would pretty much end when it was lights out. Other times I had to endure non-stop talking, singing, drum playing, crying, screaming, and snoring. Yes, snoring. It seems a prerequisite to being placed in prison is to be able to snore and fart loud. Stinky farts! There were many nights I was lucky to get an hour or two of sleep. Then there were the nightmares. As if things weren't bad enough while being awake, the nightmares were pure hell. I was almost glad when I began to lose my mind and quit dreaming all together. I also lost the ability to close my eyes and try to picture or envision an image.

JAIL

I hated when I would get bored I would have to take a nap. Naps during the day most always meant another sleepless night. At first I would just lie there at night and fight not being able to sleep. Then I started writing letters. I was fortunate that throughout my entire incarceration I never had a cell mate that my writing bothered them at night. The noise of tearing out a page to start writing another page would amplify so loud that it would wake up my cell mate sometimes. Even the noise of the pen writing on the paper would get to me. I learned to tear out 5 or so pages of paper from the pad so as to not make too much noise. Occasionally a guard would stop by and ask me if everything was okay because I'd be awake writing. They weren't asking me if I was okay out of concern—they didn't like me up writing, because it was out of the norm. Anything out of the norm bothered both the guards and inmates.

The first few days of being confined in such a tight space is pure hell. All sorts of thoughts run through your mind—even killing yourself. That's right—killing yourself! How? Not in the form of suicidal thoughts. Mostly from a sense of feeling so helpless, useless, and scared. Nothing can prepare you for the mental instability a prison can instill on a person immediately. Standing back against the far wall and running head first as hard as I could into the other CMU brick wall was an idea that came to mind, praying I would not just break my neck in the process. I learned later that many inmates had this very same idea. I had to keep a cell mate from doing this very thing once. Is this what being placed in a detention center is all about? Causing an individual to decide that life isn't worth living?

Hallucinations also began to play on my mind. I started to notice all the cracks in the brick wall that ran from the ceiling to the floor. Keep in mind, this entire structure is all concrete, steel, and metal. The weight must be phenomenal. What engineer can be sure the foundation and pilings in the ground can support such a structure? The thought of the entire building collapsing on top of me became scary.

There are the chemicals, I mean cleaning material used daily to clean the cells by the inmates. Again I was lucky to have cell mates that would do their share of cleaning the cell. Let's see—there were the blue, purple, yellow, pink, and clear plastic spray bottles with the different types of cleaner. Blue was the glass cleaner. Purple was to clean the toilet. Yellow was to mop the floor. Pink was air freshener. Clear was for whatever the other colors didn't seem to clean. The chemicals had to be watched closely by the guards because there were druggies that would sniff, snort, or drink anything they thought would give them a buzz. When a bottle went missing, it was usually in the same cell or cells of the chemical-freak inmates. Cleaning the cell was something to do, so most inmates didn't complain. The biggest problem was when someone would horde the cleaning materials, to include the 2 brooms, 2 mops, toilet paper wrappers used to wipe things down, and other cleaning supplies. There were 2 of everything, including the chemical bottles that were shared by 80 inmates to clean 40 cells and the common area. This was to make accountability of these items easy for the guards. The supplies were put out for 1 hour after breakfast, and if you didn't get to them, tough. It was another major source of arguments and fights.

Cells were open most of the day, but inmates didn't spend much time in them. The rule was only the two cell mates assigned to a cell were allowed inside the cell, but like everything else, this was almost impossible to enforce with 2 guards watching 80 grown men.

Guards would usually take action on enforcing this rule if something suspicious appeared to be going on. Actions like 2 or 3 inmates blocking the view of the guards, other inmates, and the cameras, while one inmate would go into a cell to steal anything worth stealing. Another action was if it seemed obvious inmate outlooks were posted around the POD to keep an eye on where the guards were while a few inmates smoked a cigarette or joint that had been snuck in. Fights inside cells, usually between cell mates, were scary as hell. There was nowhere for the inmate getting his ass kicked badly to escape to. The 2 guards were not about to go into the cell, as they could get trapped and attacked, too. It usually took the goon squad of about 6 to 8 guards armed with tazers and night sticks to arrive and put a stop to a cell fight. The PODs had cameras that showed most every area, so the guards watching in C2 could see when violence broke out in a POD or cell. The guards could also send out an alarm from the console for help to C2.

The doors on the cells had to be manually closed, but could be locked by the guards either by key or electronically at the guard's console. Guards could also communicate through the speaker boxes in each cell. The guards had no weapons. The odds of inmates jumping a guard and using any source of weapon on the guard being used against them far out weighed the guards having time to use them for protection.

COMMON/DINNING AREA

How can I best describe the common area? It was an open area of approximately 80 feet by 80 feet. The only two permanent things in this area were the two PAY TEL phone booths and the guard's console. There were 80 plastic lawn chairs, and about 20 3-foot round tables. There were 2 small color TVs mounted on the upstairs walkway wall. The TVs were located catty corner to each other at opposite ends of the room. One TV was suppose to be for movies, and the other TV for sports. Believe it or not, the majority of inmates would prefer to watch cartoons 24/7. TVs were supposed to be controlled by the guards, but like everything else, this was seldom the case. In fact, most guards could care less about the TVs as long as the inmates were happy and not arguing. The worst part about the TVs was the amount of noise they would generate. Picture being in a brand new building and the echoing noises that are amplified because rooms are empty. The same principle pretty much applied to the common area. So, as inmates sneakily would turn up the volume on the TV, the talking in the room would also increase. The noise in the POD would get so loud no one could hear either the TV or someone talking. I forgot to mention there were 6 larger plastic chairs at each of the TVs. These were reserved for the biggest inmates or those with the most power.

One of the worst fights I witnessed was in a TV watching area. Someone farted, and it stunk badly. Didn't matter who did it—what mattered was who the most inmates pointed out as the culprit. This poor guy probably never farted, but got the shit beat out of him, and the guards merely turned their heads to the entire incident. For guards to do so was not uncommon.

You'd think the TV that was supposed to only have sports on would be the one everyone sat around—especially the brothers. Not! Most of the time inmates would sneak and put on a soap opera, or BET, or cartoons. This area was generally where most of the ignorant and rude, loud talkers sat, the troublemakers in the POD. This was also the farthest place in the common area from the guard's console.

Entertainment in the common area was very limited. There were the two TVs. Some inmates played cards — the cards had to be bought at the commissary. Spades was by far the prominent game. Some inmates played together day-in and day-out. There were groups of 4 who played together constantly. Then there were games where the winners of 3 games would stay to play the next challengers. These almost ritualistic unwritten rules would change for various reasons. Some inmates would get tired of playing all of the time, and there was always another inmate ready to replace him. Some partners would get mad at each other and quit. Then there were always those leaving the POD for good—or hopefully for good, as I did see some return after being released. Casino was a game I learned, but it was too quick and boring. I learned some other card games, but don't remember the names of the games. I watched and learned how prison checkers was played. Too much for me to learn to play, but it passed the time to watch others play it. A few played chess—too long and boring.

I spent most of the time just sitting and people watching. I didn't have my glasses for a good while, so I couldn't read the paper or the close-caption on the TV. I had nothing in common with any of the other inmates—plus I learned, "Loose lips sink ships." Talking can get you hurt badly in prison. An inmate might be your best friend one day, so you feel like you can talk and share things with him. The next day, for any given reason, he might be your worst enemy, and then tells everyone you talked about what you said. There was no code of honor amongst prisoners or guards. I all but counted every hair on my hands just for something to do. Sitting was about all I did most days.

PRISON DINING

The common area doubled as the dining area. Inmates were locked down a half hour before food trays came. The trustees would then align the tables and chairs to make the room appear like a dining area. Food was wheeled in up front by the guard's console. Trustees were in charge of passing out the trays. I didn't eat much the first few days, if at all. I quickly learned that food, to include snacks bought at the commissary, was the most valuable commodity there is in prison. If a prisoner could sell time, they would all be millionaires—but food was a different story – it was money.

I give credit where credit is due. Some of the prison food was very good. I was never allowed to volunteer to join any of the work details, and working in the kitchen was one of the main work details. The one most visible to the public are the outdoor road cleanup crews. They wear orange-striped jump suits, as they were a security level above me and my dark-blue jump suit. The prisoners cooked the food—they were supervised, but they cooked it. Now think about this. We had 80 men in our POD, and I don't have a clue how many PODs there were in the facility. The prison must be sensitive to inmates with diabetes, who are under nourished, obese, allergic to foods, and to people of different religions, by preparing special dietary trays for them. They must also keep accountability of these folks as they come and go or are moved. Food must be filling enough to keep inmates satisfied so inmates don't become angry because they are hungry. We got 3 meals during the week and 2 meals on weekends. One guess as to when most fights broke out? Hunger probably caused the most fights.

JAIL

Breakfast was served between 6 and 6:30 a.m. depending on where one's POD was scheduled to get the meal trays. This was rotated so the different PODS would get their food at what they considered a fair time their fair share of the time. Lunch was between 11 and 11:30, and dinner was between 3 and 3:30. It was a long time between dinner and breakfast. This is why the saving of food, trading for food, and being able to buy snacks from the commissary became a major part of prison life.

I learned to guard my food using my arms and elbows around my tray. There were always the larger or powerful inmates going around snatching food off other inmate's trays. I had my food taken a few times. Nothing I could do at the time. That is where friends and alliances play a big role. Meal time was definitely the most stressful time of each day. My wife recently told me after my release how I was still guarding my food at home, with my arms out around my plate, without realizing it. Guards never got involved with what happened between inmates at meal time unless it appeared things were going to get out of hand.

So what did the meals consist of? Turkey! Inmates said everything was made out of turkey. The first couple weeks the meals weren't too bad, once I started eating. In fact, I quickly got to the point I wanted more than the portions we were being served. Another area where friendships and alliances play a major role—gradually I had my group who took care of my needs. It wasn't through intimidation, being big and bad and strong, having money, knowing other inmates, or connections with any of the guards. You will have to read on to find out the key to my success.

Breakfast was my favorite meal. We had pancakes, French toast, grits, oatmeal, cereal, toast, biscuits and gravy, jelly, and always a pint of cold milk. We didn't get a choice or all of this every morning. Our trays had 4 food slots. 2 for the main portion of a meal and 2 slots for the smaller portions. Sometimes a slot would be empty. A meal might be 2 pancakes and 2 pieces of inedible toast, with the milk. Lunch quickly became the worst meal. There were 2 combinations of lunches throughout the week days (no lunch on weekends). Peanut butter sandwiches and chips, or baloney (turkey) sandwiches and chips. 2 cookies usually were the dessert. Orange Kool-Aid or lemonade was served with every lunch. Dinners were generally good depending on the cook. They prepared chicken four different ways fried, baked, barbequed, and patties. We had a lot of meatloaf, and whether it was cooked all the way and the spices the cook used determined how good it was. There was spaghetti, beef on noodles, corn bread, garlic bread, bread, and what I thought were good desserts, usually different types of cake. They served sweet tea every dinner.

The bad parts about meals were numerous. Trays often had caked-on food from previous meals. Trays would be soaked in soapy water and not dried. Food was often slopped onto the trays. All sorts of things like finger nails, teeth, hair, and numerous other foreign items were found in the food. The food was often more than just cold. Food was often totally inedible for a variety of reasons: not cooked, over cooked, bad taste, toast so hard it would hurt your teeth, and inmates putting their hands on your food. There was also the monotony of what was available to eat. Another problem was teeth hurting. I don't know what it is, but after being in the joint for a while it seems most every inmate developed sore teeth. Didn't matter the age—it had to be something in the turkey. I left with 4 teeth crumbling that really needed to be pulled out. For some reason the prison quit providing the small salt and pepper paper packages to put on meals. Grits aren't the best food in the world without salt, pepper, and butter.

Silverware consisted of a plastic spoon. If you couldn't cut it or eat with the spoon then that is what God gave a person to use—fingers. This was not the preferred method of eating, as there wasn't a napkin provided to wipe one's hand and mouth for that matter. The jump suit was an all-purpose outfit.

The dining area was so filthy—all I every saw was a straw broom and dust pan used to sweep it up. Never saw a vacuum, or the carpet being steam cleaned. I did see food fights with trays being flung, food thrown, or being poured on an inmate and the carpet. Usually other inmates would intervene, and the inmates would get back to eating. Guards were there to make sure a POD staying under control. There were some rules, but whatever worked to keep inmates orderly is all the guards cared about. An open room with 2 guards and 80 inmates aren't the best of odds for the guards. Not all inmates were all there in the head. Some didn't care if they stayed in the place for life. They were the scary ones. I quickly learned to stay away from them.

Syrup for the pancakes and French toast was often poured from on inmate's tray to another, with a good bit spilling onto the carpet. When the tables were wiped down by the trustees after each meal they merely swiped the food remains from the table top onto the carpet. Trays were accidentally spilled onto the floor all of the time. E POD displays a 94% State Food Inspection sign. Nothing is typed on the form, and no one in the POD has ever seen a State Food Inspector in the place, but the sign has 94% written on it. Well, we never went below or above the 94% cleanliness rating. I'd also come to learn the other PODs all had a 94% health inspection rating when I was moved to B POD.

PAY TEL PHONE SYSTEM

The only connection to the outside world besides writing letters and one weekly half-hour visitation was the PAY TEL phone system inside the common area. It is also a nightmare beyond belief to use.

In order for the PAY TEL PHONE system to operate, the individual at the other end must open an account with money in it in order for a phone call to be made to that person's phone. PAY TEL gives a free 1-minute phone call to any phone number to try to explain how the system works and to get an account set up. How does an inmate learn how the system works when there are no instructions? You can't trust most of what inmates tell you, and the guards could care less. I was lucky my wife was smart enough to figure out how to contact PAY TEL and get an account set up. There is no set amount that has to be put in the account; however a 15-minute local call costs $3 and change, with taxes. Long distance calls would cost $20 or more a call. You get charged for all 15 minutes whether all the minutes are used or not. There were several times when an inmate would get mad and hang up before the 15 minutes were up. A message would come over the line letting you know there were 25 seconds remaining on that call. That was about the only nice thing about PAY TEL. This did give one time to at least say, "I love and miss you, dear," before the call was terminated. All of this I had to learn over time.

There were a total of 8 of these phones, 4 phones to each phone both. The booths were centered in middle of the common area. There was no privacy while talking. The TVs and loud talking made trying to talk on the phone very frustrating. Plus the reception over the phone was so poor one usually had to yell to be heard. The same from the person on the other end, as the sound level would waver in and out.

Morning was the best time to call, as the POD was quieter, and even the TVs were turned down some, so hearing wasn't such a problem. When my wife first put money into a PAY TEL account I was calling her 3 times a day. Sometimes I would make back-to-back calls, just to hear her voice. Then the money would run out on the account quickly, and I would have to wait until our weekly half-hour visit to talk to her.

Calls could become heated for several reasons, especially when I was trying to convey important information to my wife about my case, and she couldn't hear me, or vice versa. The whole system was frustrating.

There were always broken phones from inmates getting frustrated and mad and breaking them. These phones were solid, but when a powerful inmate gets mad—well, I saw a phone get totally yanked off the stand more than once. Guards were always slow to get a new phone installed or repaired. Usually inmates would sit and pound on the push numbers with the solid plastic receiver until the metal push numbers would break.

I saw one fight, or sort of a fight, occur over the use of the phones. It was hard to even get to a phone in the evening, as that was when most inmates would call. Some had several accounts and could sit at a phone for an hour or more. Most of the time only 4 of the 8 phones would be working. I later found out this was done by the prison, the fact only 4 of the phones worked, because when I changed to go live in B POD the phones were enabled the same way. Now when a phone got torn out of the panel I witnessed guards fixing them. So why weren't all of the phones fixed? Guards didn't like the phones, anyways, as they did frustrate inmates more than they helped.

Back to the outbreak between 2 inmates over the phones. Certain phones seemed to work better than others. These 2 inmates had been sitting waiting for a guy to finish talking so they could use that same phone. When the inmate finished with his call the two guys waiting both got to the phone at the same time. First a verbal exchange began. It wasn't long before they were wrestling around on the floor. Other inmates were able to separate them, and no blows were thrown. In fact, these 2 inmates were buddies. When a ruckus would break out and didn't amount to much, the guards would usually just put the ones involved in lock-down in their cells. That is what happened this time.

Guards would seldom let inmates go to in-take to make an outside call free on a prison phone. There was an occasional emergency, or if an inmate was in really tight with a guard, they would be allowed to go make a free call. I did get to go make one phone call at in-take to my wife, but it wasn't by choice. Things had built up in her to the point that during one of the periods we didn't have any money in our PAY TEL account she keep calling the prison. I was called up by one of the guards and told they were going to let me call her at in-take this one time, but I would be in some sort of trouble if she persisted in calling in the future. Fortunately for me, she never called them again.

Another problem with the PAY TEL phones was the seats were all metal. Fifteen minutes of sitting on metal might not sound like much, but when you sat all day long, your ass was sensitive to anything. Sometimes I'd be in so much pain sitting in that chair I almost told my wife good-bye and hung up. I'd even go so far as to tie my long-john shirt around my butt to make it like a little cushion to sit on. Why didn't I just move around, get a plastic chair to sit in, or stand-up? Because the metal cord was only about 2 feet long. You could barely change ears while talking. I also remember my hands hurting so badly from holding on so hard to the receiver for 15 minutes. It would take several minutes for me to just open my hands, as they hurt so badly. I hate PAY TEL, and there aren't many things I absolutely hate in life.

Three-way calls were illegal and punishable. Never knew of anyone being punished for making one, but it was done all of the time. I'd never heard of PAY TEL and never want to hear the name again. Inmates talked about suing for any and everything, but this is one business I think needs to be sued. The hell with being sued—they need to be put out of business for good. Then some other company would just move in and rip off the inmates, or inmates would go without phones to call loved ones. Nobody really cares.

TRUSTEES

Trustees were inmates selected to assist the guards in whatever capacity is required. Some were even selected from the actual prison to come serve their time as a trustee.

Trustees had a lot of responsibilities, one being the attitude of the inmates in the POD. Another was keeping everything as neat, clean, organized, and done in an orderly and fair manner. This helped to keep inmates calm most of the time. Some inmates were just plain mean, ignorant, abusive, have no manners, and are always looking for trouble. Trustees hated this type of inmate, and so did most of the other inmates.

Meals, linen exchange, changing jump suits, and clean up in the morning and night were trustees' primary responsibilities. Trustees were responsible for assisting guards with new inmates and inmates leaving. Assisting the guards as needed was another.

It might not sound like much, but doing these things day in and day out got old. So why would an inmate want to be a trustee? There were some perks for being a trustee. Those who were considered permanent trustees got time off for good behavior. Time off was usually 2 days for 1 towards their sentence. In certain cases, an inmate could even be given three days for one. Another perk was getting to watch TV while all the other inmates were in lock-down. This could get ugly, as many inmates liked to take naps during lock-down just to pass the time away. Sometimes a trustee liked to put country music on TV, turn it up loud, and sing (usually very poorly to the songs), and play the drums on a table or chair. This could get on anyone's nerves quickly. This was usually a stunt pulled by a volunteer trustee.

Volunteer trustees came and went almost daily. They assisted the main trustees with serving the meals, cleaning, and whatever else was needed. I once volunteered to be a trustee. This was the one evening I cleaned the showers. It was the only time I was a trustee.

Trustees, for the most part, blended in with the other inmates. There were some trustees that liked to show they were privileged, but what goes around, comes around. Trustees often needed assistance, whether doing some work or for personal assistance, so they didn't want to burn bridges with the other inmates for the most part. Some of the trustees would help new inmates get adjusted to being in jail, help older inmates get food and medicine, and would help inmates in general. Others, you wouldn't know they were in the place, sleeping or keeping to themselves. There were a few trustees that harassed certain inmates or caused trouble in general. These trustees would ultimately cause enough trouble for guards that they would end up losing their position. Each trustee was an individual with his own personality.

Another perk being a trustee was to have something to do to pass the day away. Being a trustee was not a full-time job by any means, but being called upon to do odd jobs beats just sitting around all day long.

One of the biggest perks was meals, and getting the extra food on trays that no one claims. Usually there were an average of 5 or so extra trays per meal. This can be from inmates that didn't want their food to eat, to the kitchen not being told an inmate had left the POD. There was a case when an inmate left, and was gone for weeks, but the kitchen keep sending his tray because there was a new inmate that came with the same name. He was added to the list of inmates, but the guards didn't take the other inmate off. On top of that, the inmate that left was a diabetic, and diabetics got a special snack bag each evening. The trustees would share this bag at evening. It consisted of a sandwich, a bag of Lays potato chips, and a pint of milk.

The term for inmates without any money to buy stamps, pen, envelopes, or paper, is an "indentured" inmate. An inmate had to be there 7 days before qualifying for an indentured inmate package of items. The inmate also had to submit an inmate request form to get the package. I had qualified as being indentured, but no one told me I had to fill out the form, so I never got my package. Often times an inmate would leave and his indentured package would finally arrive. Trustees shared these as well. There were these, and some other perks that made being either a main trustee or a volunteer trustee appealing, but none of it appealed to me.

It was a good idea to get on the good side of the main trustees, and even better if you could get to be friends. There were times when a trustee could have some influence over the decision of a guard. Trustees were most always in a position of providing a friend with extra food or drinks at meal time. Inmates would always be giving trustees snacks for favors. Trustees would often have so many snacks they would share them with inmates they liked. I was generally able to make friends with most all the inmates and the trustees.

I wasn't big on snacks, and tried not to be a nuisance to anyone by asking for any type of favor unless I really needed one. The head trustee in B POD and I became pretty good friends. He would watched over me, having high blood pressure himself. He'd most always make sure I got enough food. He even got to know the foods I liked and would get me extra portions. There were a couple of times I missed pill call. He was able to use his influence to get the guard to let me go down to the nurse's station to get my medicine. I'd offer him snacks, but we both knew he had plenty and had to watch his weight. He liked talking to me. We were the same age, and about the two most educated individuals in the POD. Occasionally, there would be an inmate you could tell had a very high IQ, but they usually were strange or nerdy. You didn't overdo things, or they would become boring. This trustee and I didn't spend a whole lot of time talking. It was more like quality time for us to talk.

This particular trustee in B POD had a counterpart that also come over from the prison for the 2-days-for-1-day credit. This trustee was something else. I found out later that he was the one who stole my snacks from my box.

There were trustees I just plain couldn't stand. I would tend to just stay away from inmates I didn't care for, but this jerk trustee just wouldn't leave me alone. It didn't take a rocket scientist to figure out the dude was trouble. He just knew someone in the right place and was selected to be a trustee. All I could figure out was that since the main trustee seemed to like me, he wanted to buddy up with me. He seemed to always be interrogating me about any and everything. I was really glad when he finally left.

There was one very strange trustee. He only came out of his cell when it was time to eat or time to do his job of evening clean up. He was incarcerated before I got there, and was still there when I left. No one knew much about him, other than he stayed in his cell all of the time doing nothing. He didn't even read books. There were inmates who chose to stay in their cells much of the time, but they were usually book readers.

HYGIENE

Hygiene was probably one of the most serious and scariest issues while in prison. Guys came into the place with sores and scabs all over their bodies. I learned heavy methamphetamine users developed sores that scab up all over their bodies. Inmates developed sores and scabs that they constantly picked at. There was one large black inmate with corn rolls. He had sores all over his head that had scabbed up to the size of a silver dollar. All he would do is sit and pick at them all day long. It was gross. And guess where all those scabs fell to—the carpet. All the guards and inmates were constantly picking at a scab or sore. Nurses carried creams in their push carts that were supposed to help dry up and clear up sores, but they were as stingy with passing these out as they were with any other medicine.

There was one older inmate brought in. He was wearing his flip flops and had no socks. The guards told him to go stand in a corner. One look and you could tell he wasn't all there mentally. He started pacing in a circle. His feet were a mess. He had open sores and scabs on his feet. Puss was oozing and blood was coming from these sores on his feet, and he continued to walk about. His toenails were very long. So long they curled up in the air. The man also had sores all over his face. After a while he was out of his corner trying to mingle with other inmates. No one wanted to be near him. The problem now was he was infecting the carpet with his open sores. The man was finally taken out of the POD, to everyone's delight. Unbelievably, this same inmate was returned to our POD a few days later. He still had all the sores, and wandered aimlessly about.

JAIL

Fortunately, once again he was removed from the POD. What all in the prison facilities had he infected, and with what? Where was the medical help for this man, both physically and mentally?

Trustees were responsible for keeping the place clean, but had to constantly solicit volunteers to help them. I've talked about wiping the food off table after meals onto the carpet. The cleaning of the entire place was done just as sloppily. I volunteered to clean showers because I was sick and tired of how filthy they were. Hairs, snot on the walls, wrappers for the little soaps, shampoo bottles, and most everything filthy made its way to the showers. There were paint chips (I'm sure some got eaten) and cracks in the walls and floor. Cleaning the showers took place during the 10 p.m. lock-down. There were about 6 inmates helping the guards get the common area ready for the next day. Other duties besides cleaning the showers were to clean the 1 toilet room, mopping the floors without carpet, sweep the carpet with a straw broom, cleaning the guard's console area, cleaning the multipurpose room, and cleaning the recreation room. The place really got a good scrubbing in 15 minutes—NOT!

I'd gotten the purple chemical bottle that was used to clean the shower floors and walls, and the industrial-bristle broom. I'd just got started on the first of 8 shower stalls when the trustee came up to me and asked what in the hell I was doing? I told him I was cleaning the showers. He said at the rate I was going I would be up all night, and so would all the other workers—we all had to stay out until the cleaning material were all accounted for, put away, and then we could go to our cells for the night. I will admit I'm no dummy and knew all of this. What I was doing was making a statement the showers needed more cleaning, and they did—really bad. He also told me I was using too much of the chemical, and was costing the prison money—like he really cared. He just wanted me to get done and move on. He went on to tell me to clean the shower stalls on the floor my cell was on since those were the ones I would be using. I told him I preferred a shower stall up stairs. He shrugged his shoulders in disgust and walked away. A little while later the guard flashed the lights as a signal for us to start bringing the cleaning material to be put away. Also for the inmates in their cells it was 10 minutes until lights out for the night.

While putting up my cleaning material, I (jokingly to myself) told the trustee how much I enjoyed cleaning and was looking forward to the next evening. With a look as serious as he could muster, he told me I did a great job. He knew I had high blood pressure, and told me to give it a break for a while. He would let me know when he thought it would be time for me to help him again. He never did ask me to help again. I was glad, as it disgusted me even more to actually get down to see all the filth in the shower drains, and try to get the shit out.

Another gross thing, most all inmates constantly did was to sit and pick their noses. Remember, there is not even a paper towels in the common toilet to wipe your hands, so where did these boogers go? Into the carpet! Some inmates were nice enough to eat their boogers. The jump suit and arm was about the only thing available to wipe snort. You could always tell an inmate with a cold, because the dark blue jump suit would gradually begin to turn white from all the snot—or the inmate was just a filthy individual. Then inmates would walk around shaking hands, and touching each other. So as not to touch one another there is a special prison handshake.

Speaking of filthy individuals—there were plenty of them. It was pretty much known who showered and who didn't. This was something inmates paid close attention to. It should be the responsibility of the guards to make sure inmates stayed clean and washed sometimes. There were individuals who would wash themselves in their cells with the wash rag, soap, and using the sink. It was their business. Saying someone didn't shower was also one way of getting the other inmates pissed off at that person. Even if everyone saw that inmate take showers, if someone said they didn't shower, then it was true. This would usually lead to inmates picking on that person or verbally abusing them—never saw a fight I knew over not taking a shower.

Not exchanging your jump suit was another thing inmates tended to keep track of. When you live with individuals almost 24/7, it becomes obvious if they are wearing the same jump suit all of the time. Jump suits were too much for the personal washer and dryers, and would take forever to dry if you tried to wash a suit in a cell, so the only way was to change. Some guards would let inmates take a new jump suit to their cells to try on to make sure they fit, didn't have too many stains, and to make sure the snaps worked. It also provided a little privacy, especially for the inmates without any underwear—I was one of those for a few weeks. Other guards, male or female, would make inmates go 3 at a time into the multi-purpose room to exchange suits. No luxury of trying them on to check them out. You got what the trustee gave you. Some jump suits were in such bad shape guards would allow them to be swapped, but the suit had to either been a really bad fit or was in really bad shape. A jump suit was critical, because if it didn't fit, or had too much starch, or whatever, it could easily rub sores on your body that could get serious. Remember, an inmate wears that jump suit 24/ 7.

I mentioned both male and female guards would be in the multi-purpose room while inmates were changing out jump suits? Some inmates did not have underwear on. If you are concerned about modesty then you better not go to prison. Showering was the same way. Both male and female guards would position themselves so they could view into the shower areas while inmates were taking showers. What could an inmate do? An inmate had better not gun (shake his dick) at a guard either. The punishment for gunning a guard was usually solitary confinement in one's cell. The longest lock-down I knew of was 4 to 8 hours.

Unhealthy hygiene was everywhere in prison. I already talked about the food trays, and the surprises in the food, such as finger nails, teeth, and unknowns, but the carpet just totally made me sick. That carpet had never been cleaned since the building had been there.

RECREATION AREA

The recreation area was by far the most dangerous place in the entire POD. Not only did most fights break out in this area, but bad injuries were also common. This was originally designed for a smoke-break area. The electronic lighters mounted on the wall were still there, but disabled—supposedly. The room was entirely concrete and had small, 3-foot-high stages at each end. Must have been where weights were stored at one time. The room had been converted into a very small basketball area and recreation room. All the weights and such had been removed from the entire facility. Inmates would do crunches, sit-ups and such most anywhere—and most inmates were buffed! The prison paid for the basketball and net. I use to be quite a good basketball player. This was one of the ways I gained respect quick. I was too old and afraid of getting injured to play in any of the 3-on-3 games. There were a lot of good players. There were also inmates close to 7 feet in height, so games often got intense. It was hard to play in the Bob Barker flip flops. The entire room had windows so the guards could see, although there were no cameras in this area. So guess what—this was where most of the smoking cigarettes and pot, and the fights occurred. Once again, the guards would not enter the room to breakup a fight—they would wait until the goons arrived. There were often times no inmates would be there, and I would go in and just shoot. I got noticed quickly as a good shooter. On occasion, I would play Around the World, the game, 21, and some Horse—but mostly just enjoyed the peacefulness of being alone in the room just shooting the ball.

JAIL

I've mentioned before that not everything is what it appears to be, nor is everything used for its original purpose. Basketballs were no different. I saw a basketball used for every conceivable thing except to play basketball. They would have contests for who could slam the ball on the concrete floor and hit the 12-foot ceiling the most times. Guys would kick the ball as hard as they could. They would do the Michael Jordan—Larry Bird commercial of shooting from every conceivable place and position. Some of these shots were amazing, and I guess that was part of playing basketball. One of the favorite shots I learned was to throw the ball over my head, against a side wall, and ricochet the ball into the basket.

You had to pay attention to what was going on in the recreation room, even while watching, because it was easy to get hurt by balls flying out of control or by your getting slammed to the concrete floor or running into concrete the stages. There were also steps with sharp edges. There were fights over fouls or lying about scores. Most anything could set a fight off. I broke a few fingernails and incurred some other minor injuries with the little activity I did just shooting the basketball. These minor injuries created enough pain for me that I quit going in to even shoot the ball. I would go into the room sometimes to get away from the noise, warm up a bit, or just talk to an inmate. The only other reason I went in there was when our Bible Study group grew so large we couldn't fit into the multi-purpose room, and we would use the recreation area. Surprisingly, not one inmate objected, nor did any try to disrupt these sessions.

I did have one major scare personally. There were about 4 of us in the room. Out of the blue I was told to go watch the guards as a look out. The other 3 had come into the room to smoke whatever they had. I didn't care what. Being a watch out was as punishable as taking part. I just wanted to run out of the room, but there would be repercussions of some sort later. My body froze. About that time some other inmates came into the recreation room. I was able to walk out without worry. The situation was over.

MULTI-PURPOSE ROOM

The name of this room is self explanatory—this room was used for a wide variety of things: linen exchange, exchanging jump suits, storing food trays for inmates gone for a while. The primarily use for the room was for religious gatherings.

Linen exchange took place twice a week—Monday and Friday. Most inmates would turn in all three items—sheet, towel, and a wash cloth. Some preferred to keep the ones they had and would hand wash them in the sink in their cell. Some would be allowed by a trustee to use the personal washer and dryer in the POD. I would occasionally keep what I had for a period, naturally cleaning them, because sometimes you get real rags with holes, very rough on the body, and all sorts of stains. Blankets were exchanged once a month. Jump suits were exchanged twice weekly—the same days as linens. The same went for keeping a jump suit. Upon initial appearance jump suits all appeared to be alike. Far from it! Like when you go canoeing—you don't pick the nice, new, shinny canoes— they look new for a reason. They have high seats and tip over easy. You select a decent-looking used canoe—no guarantee you still won't tip over. New suits were heavier than the older suits merely because they haven't been worn and washed. Most new suits came with an elastic band around the mid section. This could become painful even to the point of rubbing raw places one's body. The elastic band could also be uncomfortable to sleep on. There were also problems with older suits. For some reason most of the older suits the bottom was torn up. A person could trip or the suit would snag onto something. The snaps, as the jump suits didn't have buttons, often didn't work. Especially the snaps around one's private parts. That was really bad if you couldn't afford boxers. They often had rips, tears, and holes. Stains were another nasty thing. Getting a jump suit that fit is also a challenge. It seemed like each jump suit was made by a different pattern. I would hang onto a good jump suit for a week, maybe two.

Religious activities were the major use of the small room. About 15 inmates could be seated fairly comfortably in the room. We had 3 folks from the outside allowed to come 3 times a week. The preacher would come on Sunday for church services. On Mondays, we had a missionary visit. On Thursdays, we had a deacon of a church visit. Each of these visits were monitored by the guards from outside and lasted 1 hour each. The services had to be controlled, and most all of the speaking was done by the guest. Each of these visitors had to undergo a good bit of background checking to be allowed to come in. These clergymen were the only outsiders allowed into a POD. We also had "Prayer Call" each evening. This was composed of inmates only. We would have about a 10 to 20 minute prayer call before evening lock-down. The number of individuals varied, but towards the end of my time we constantly had a large group of 15 or more of the total 80 inmates. Jailhouse religion is a very real and powerful happening.

VISITATION

Visitation was my most cherished time in prison. Believe it or not, some inmates did not want any visitors. My wife came mostly on Wednesdays from 1 to 4 p.m. Since she wasn't working, that worked out best for her. Tuesday visitation was from 8 a.m. to 12 noon, and Friday visitation was from 6 p.m. to 10 p.m. Having these different hours allowed those visitors who worked different schedules the opportunity to visit without taking time off from work or not be able to visit.

When my wife would arrive a guard would call out my name and let me out to walk the hall to the visitation room. There were always the same 2 female guards. They sat on the side of the wall in the room for the inmates to monitor the room. These guards grunted pretty much when they spoke to me in the beginning, but as time went on their greetings became more of, "Hey, glad to see you are getting to see your wife today."

My wife wasn't always able to come. The first time she drove all the way there, about a 45-minute drive. She was rudely turned away by the guards because I had not given her birth date to verify she was who she said she was. No one told me that I had to provide them with her birth date. Before that happened, she didn't even have a clue where the facility was. Neither did most local people. The prison complex was located way out in the boonies. Politicians found a well hidden, secluded piece of land to build the facilities on. Poor inmates who didn't have anyone to pick them up when they got released would get shoved out the door at this place by the guards. I would not of had any clue which direction to go if that had happened to me. There was a gas station about a mile down the road, I'd heard mentioned by inmates who'd been there before, and inmates released had to walk down to the gas station. They said local truck drivers were accustomed to prisoners walking there, and often give them a ride on into town. The prisoner was on his own if he didn't have a place to go to. There were some inmates that were arrested on the Interstate and didn't have anyone or any means of getting to anywhere.

I was always worried Tuesday evening about my wife coming to visit on Wednesday. We'd had a drought for the last several years, and now were having heavy thunderstorms almost every day. I'd made her promise not to come visit me even if there was just a chance of rain. God smiled on us most of the time, as the sun was out most every Wednesday. She only missed a couple of visitations after we figured the system out. She came once on a Tuesday, as we had a friend who worked at the prison. This friend happened to have to come out to get something that day from the prison. She told my wife to ride with her, as she would have time for my wife to visit me for half an hour.

Then there was our worry about our truck. We didn't have any money, and all of a sudden the truck had started needing small repairs. I got mad at her when I got released that she never had new windshield wipers put on like she'd promised me. There was also the cost of gas. This all happened when new taxes on gas sky rocketed the price per gallon nation wide. The prices of a barrel of crude oil was up above $120. I think gas was reaching the $3.00 price range. It didn't always seem that God was smiling on us; however, the cost of gas did keep her off roads even in town. The roads in this region are very dangerous. I now look at this price rise in gas prices as a blessing in disguise.

The visitation room was shaped like a hallway with a wall dividing the room. One side of the room was for the inmates to sit, and the other for the visitor or visitors to sit. My wife was the only visitor I ever had. Later I found out some good friends of mine from work had tried to visit, but again, the guards didn't have their names and birth date provided. No one tells an inmate this type of information. An inmate is inhumanely kept as isolated as humanly possible from the outside world. We were not even allowed to watch local news. Other inmates had family and friends to come visit. Like everything else, if you were a good inmate, the guards would let you have more than one half-hour visit a week. There were about 12 stalls in the room with a glass pane separating you. In the pane was a small piece of metal to talk into. The glass was usually filthy and hard to see through. The seats were little metal seats, just like the PAY TEL phone seats, to sit on for half an hour. Once again I learned to tie my long-john shirt around my waist under my jump suit to use as a little extra cushion to sit on. My wife learned to bring a sweater or coat to sit on.

When the room was full it got hard to hear what each other was trying to say. This got very frustrating when you were trying to convey information pertinent to one's case. More than once I left with a headache and very frustrated. I often wanted to stand up and yell out to others to shut up, because many would get ignorant and talk like they were the only ones visiting in the room. I still always cherished every second to gaze into my wife's beautiful blue eyes and face—not to mention her gorgeous body.

This was also the only opportunity in prison to get a chance to gaze out the windows behind where my wife would sit and see the sun, blue skies, and clouds. If I got real lucky, a flock of birds might fly by.

THE COMMISSARY

The time of the week every lucky inmate with money in his account looked forward to was going to the commissary. This was done twice a week. E POD's days were Tuesday and Thursday. Other inmates from other PODs were seldom in the same place at the same time— especially the female inmates. Passing in the hall way was about the only time to see an inmate in a different-colored jump suit or a female. Inmates were required to walk on the right side (the grey tiles) of the hall way. Talking or signing was not permitted. This was monitored by the guards sitting in the command and control (C2)rooms with total visibility to the long, straight hallways. Usually a verbal warning was enough to keep an inmate under control, but sometimes the guards would have to take some action, and the inmate would usually get 24hour lock-down in his cell.

Once my family found out about my being in prison, and what was going on, they sent money. It was always enough to get me what I needed. I'm not much of a snack eater anyway. The first thing I bought was an extra-large long-john shirt—they didn't sell the bottoms. Then I got the tee shirts, boxers, socks, soap, toothbrush, pen, paper, envelopes, and stamps. Oh—I also bought a few snacks. I came to enjoy the Danish Cheese Cake and Snyder's Jalapeño Pretzels. They were hard to find. My teeth hurt me, so the sweet of the Danish, and the hardness of the pretzels made them less enjoyable to eat. Most everyone bought some mints, mostly to share with other inmates with foul breath.

The way the commissary operated was, the evening before "Store Call" a computer sheet would be placed under your cell door by one of the guards.

It would have your name and how much money was in your account. I got one sheet for 5 cents—which was enough buy one envelope. Hell—I traded the envelope for a cake at dinner to an inmate who wanted an envelope that bad. Other inmates had a few thousand dollars on their account. Some guards passed the commissary sheets out right after lock-down for the evening at 10 p.m. allowing an inmate to fill out what items he would be buying the next day. That was always better than getting the form at some outrageous time in the early hours of the morning, and trying to figure out what you wanted. The print was so small it often took team work with other inmates to read what an item was or the price. There was the flimsy refill of a pen to try and write with. I'd become pretty good using my pen. Some store sheets looked like they'd been through a war by the time an inmate had made up his mind as to what he wanted.

Mostly the commissary had all sorts of small bags of chips, candy bars, sweet rolls, mints, Lifesavers, large cookies, packages of cookies, salami, salami and cheese, peanut butter and jelly, crackers, and other small food items. The prices were a total rip off, but better than not having something to buy. There was the underwear, pens, paper, envelopes, and stamps to buy. Holiday and birthday cards were also available. There were necessities for the female inmates too. There was also a wide variety of Bob Barker and other toiletry items available. Most of these were not supposed to be sold—some even having the statement on the item. Oh—I almost forgot the favorite item by far—each inmate could get one soda. Just one soda per inmate, and the bottles were carefully monitored by the guards. Soda bottles could be used for all sorts of things like squirting feces or urine at a guard.

I didn't get to experience a trip to the commissary for almost a month. During this time I hadn't established enough of a rapport with any inmates for any of them to share snacks with me. I didn't mind not having the extra food until I started getting it. In fact, I had a really bad experience my first store trip. I bought all the necessities I'd mentioned, plus a few chocolate candy bars (Milky Way, Three Musketeers, and a Payday). After eating about half of one I began to feel really ill. I buzzed the guard on the intercom that I was ill—we were under evening lock-down at the time. After my numerous attempts at telling the guard I was ill, my cell mate finally demanded I get medical attention. I finally did. I got to walk down the hall to the nurse's station. The nurse on duty finally did a blood sugar stick pin in my finger, had me wait about 30 minutes and did it again. She told me I was borderline low blood sugar and would be just fine. She gave me a miniature Snickers bar and sent me back to the POD. I gave my cell mate the rest of the candy, and it was a while before I tried another candy bar.

It was nice to get out of the POD to walk down the hall and sit for 30 or so minutes waiting for your name to be called and to go up to the counter to get your snacks and other items. The lead inmate of the group would collect the forms from each inmate as we entered a small waiting room with about 12 plastic chairs in it.

There was a $100 limit on an inmate spending each trip to the Commissary, and there were 2 days each week to go to the commissary (to have store call). I saw individuals buy as much as 3 over-flowing brown paper garbage bags full of junk food. These individuals were called the "POD Store", and in the POD had a lot of power—that is, while they had the money and the snacks. Food was money in prison. If you weren't big and bad, then you'd better have money for food to ensure protection.

The biggest problem inside the POD was when an inmate had both the size and the money. These inmates were generally the ones that would dictate how the POD operated, even to the point of having control over the guards. There was one other class of inmate with the same type of power, and those were the long timers with all the prison smarts. Trading now took on an entirely different style. Prison food could be traded for snacks or other store-bought material. Snacks could be traded for most anything, to include protection. Having snacks would just bring on an entirely different persona for inmates with them. An inmate might be craving a candy bar so bad he might trade an entire meal for one candy bar. The problem is, about a short time later that inmate would become hungry. Hunger quickly turns into an attitude, and attitudes can lead to violence. Guards tried to keep this type of trading from occurring, but keeping an eye on 80 men eating at one time is all but impossible. Weekends were the worst, as we only got two meals, and the portions are no different from other meals during the week. For an inmate to trade a meal on a weekend was most assuredly cause for trouble that day.

Sharing—surprisingly most inmates displayed better manners and more sharing than people in general. If an inmate knew another was hungry and hadn't stupidly traded away his meal, they would share what they had. They wouldn't just break off a small piece of a candy bar or whatever—they often gave most of candy bar.

JAIL

Some inmates had money to buy so many snacks that they seldom ate the prison food. I saw some inmates go for months without coming to eat at meal time. They were allowed to eat their snacks in their cells; otherwise the other inmates would hound them for some of their snacks. There was also a major problem with these inmates with food and snacks. All the other inmates knew who is in which cell, and those with an abundance of snacks. I witnessed these inmates with their Tupperware box full of snacks wiped out, and have to wait until the next store call to stock up. I had my snacks stolen once. It is not a good feeling. It generates fear and the sense of vulnerability while in the POD. I got over it—sort of—but it took a while.

ICE BUCKET TREAT

Remember when you were a kid and you'd hear the music down the block signaling the ice cream truck was just a few houses away? You'd rush home to get enough money for an ice cream, and rush back hoping to be the first one in line. That was about the same way with the ice bucket when it was brought into the POD.

It was a 5-gallon, round, ice bucket full of crushed ice. You'd think the bucket was full of the best ice in the world. Inmates would sit around the area where the bucket would be placed, like they weren't going to get any. They'd be poised with their plastic cup in hand, and ready to fight if any of the other inmates even appeared to be trying to get in front of them.

What was so special about this ice? Nothing—it was just like any other ice. No coloring or flavor. The ice bucket would be brought in 3, sometimes 4 times a day. It came after each meal, and sometimes an extra bucket would be brought in the evening.

There would be a plastic scoop and rubber gloves to get the ice out. Most of the time inmates would dip their cup into the bucket or use their hands to get ice. The bucket always was taken out of the POD empty. Guys would hold the bucket up and tip it to get that last piece of ice.

I wasn't real big on getting the ice, as the cold and hardness of the ice would hurt my teeth. On occasion I'd get some for ice water, but even ice-cold water hurt my teeth. A bucket of ice was the jail-house treat. Another example of how the little things we take for granted come to mean so much to a person in prison—ice!

HEALTHCARE

What an experience healthcare is in prison. I hardly know where to start, because this was my biggest problem from the very beginning. As I've already mentioned, I spent most of my first 8 hours in a small cell called "the hole." The in-processing guard never completed the medical portion of my file. It took me days to get any sort of blood-pressure medicine and almost a month for them to finally allow my wife to bring my doctor's prescription medicine. The so-called nurses would only give me 1 of my 2 medicines I'd been taking for almost 30 years. Nurses came to each of the PODs twice a day. For me to get my medicine the four times a day as prescribed would generate more work for them. A nurse had me sign a waiver stating that if I wanted my blood pressure medicine the four times a day I would have to be put in solitary confinement 24/7. Needless to say, at 52 years old, suffering with very high blood pressure, it is a wonder I am here writing this right now.

I was born with a heart murmur, and at the age of 20 was put on the blood-pressure medicine after a serious car accident. I was able to play all sports, but with my age catching up to me, not being given the proper doses of my medicine was the last thing I needed. Prison was stressful enough without high blood pressure. The few times the nurses attempted to take my blood pressure, the top and bottom numbers were always sky high. That was except for one nurse. She would not put the arm band on securely and would barely squeeze the pump to attempt to get an accurate reading. Her reading always showed I had low blood pressure. When I say high blood pressure, I am talking about 200 over 110.

JAIL

Doctors consider these blood pressure numbers potential stroke level. With my medicine taken as prescribed would average 120 over 80.

Being in prison is stressful enough—the surroundings—the drastic change in lifestyle—food—the type of people you're surrounded by—noise—pain—metal bed—boredom—and that list goes on and on. The most stressful part of prison was being on total alert at all times. A cell mate can lose his mind at any time while you are confined in the room with him. Fights can break out at anytime over most anything. I already mentioned a terrible fight over a fart. Another was over a paperback book (another high-value commodity in prison). I saw gang fights. Fights would break out over basketball games. I've mentioned fights over food and hunger, but gambling for food is a topic all of its own. One had to constantly be aware of one's surroundings and what was happening in every direction. I witnessed a guard tackle two inmates, and take out four others sitting at the table where the event happened all in one swoop. I've mentioned inmates fighting in their cells while they were in lock-down and the guards ignoring what was happening. I witnessed one big black guy totally pummel a small Mexican mafia member. Gangs weren't prevalent where I was, as it was a detention facility. (A detention center is usually a place where inmates are awaiting trial to determine their ultimate fate or place they will be going to.) This type of stress was even harder for me to deal with, daily having high blood pressure, and not getting my proper medication.

The sound of a sneeze or cough would send chills through an inmate for fear of getting sick. Being sick in prison is hell. I had my 1 experience of being sick. For a couple of days I knew I was coming down with something, and like they say, sickness always seems to get worse at nighttime. About the third day I was sick. Fortunately my cell mate was known by the guard, and he was a real nurse. He finally told the guard over the intercom that I was running a fever and needed medical attention immediately. Once again we were in lock-down, and it was about midnight. The nurse came and sure enough, I had a temperature of 101 degrees. She took me to the nurses' station.

The nurses' station consisted of a waiting room with about 15 chairs. This room had about 4 offices used primarily to interview new inmates. I think there were 2 observation rooms with hospital-style beds. The adjoining room was where the nurses stayed, all the medicine and equipment was kept, and there were about 8 rooms for patients. There was an armed guard between these two rooms 24/7. There were nurses on staff 24 hours a day. I never did see a doctor or dentist. I think there were 3 or 4 nurses on each 12-hour shift. Their primary job was to get the medications ready and distributed to the inmates in all of the PODs. I must admit they had one heck of job to perform; my problem was wondering just how qualified they were. Some of the things they would say or do, I felt a candy striper would be more qualified.

I became a patient for 2 days when I came down with this illness. The room was smaller than a cell, as they were for one inmate. The metal bed was a little larger, and at first the mattress seemed a little thicker with a larger lump for a pillow. I was allowed to bring my blanket, by now I'd been in the place long enough to have obtained a hospital blanket. They were larger and softer. The nurse gave me two aspirin and told me I'd have to keep the blanket off and probably remove my jump suit. She finally came right out and accused me of intentionally doing everything in my power to get my temperature up.

The food was identical to what were served in the POD. Feeling ill I didn't eat much while there. The nurses would come around to give me my 2 aspirin as I was getting to sleep. I still got my blood pressure medicine twice a day, as I'd signed that waiver, and they didn't want to start a precedence with me getting the meds 4 times a day.

The cell had a toilet and sink. The shower was in a separate room, but only had cold water. This nurse's area was freezing. I don't know what I would have done if they had forced me to keep my blanket off, and to remove my jump suit—I did have my boxers, tee shirt, and socks at the time. Thank God my fever broke the second day. I was ready to get back to the POD.

These nurses did have a very difficult job. Like the food, pill call varied some from day to day. Then there were times when a medicine nurse would have to respond to an emergency, and we'd have to wait. This could take hours for me to get my medicine.

Medicines came around twice a day. Usually the times were around 8 a.m. and 8 p.m. This was forever for me, as I really needed my medicine the 4 times a day. Some days I didn't think I was going to make it until the nurse came. When "Pill Call!" was yelled out, and it wasn't always yelled out, you'd better be ready to get your medicine. The hardest time was the evening pills, as there was always a lot going on then. Showers were only allowed in the evening, and the showers were at the very back, where it was hard to hear. Hell—with the TVs blaring and everyone talking at the top of their lungs in the evening made it difficult to always be ready for the nurse. The nurses were not on a set schedule. Having inmate friends paid off for me. On several occasions I'd have friends running around to find me to make sure I got my meds. Most of the time I'd be in the shower. Heck—one time I was sitting right where the nurse came in with her cart and passed out the meds. It was so loud that I missed her and had to wait until morning until I got my meds.

Let me tell more about the procedure so you have a better picture as to how all of this was taking place. Things are never on a consistent time schedule, and for me, getting my blood pressure medicine was more important than the food. Everyone knows when the food arrives, as most everyone is ready to eat. There were only a handful of inmates getting medicine. Most of the other inmates could care less. They were more concerned about the TV show or whatever they were doing. The nurse would arrive with her push cart. The cart consisted of pills with those of us with documented medical issues from our private doctors. The cart also had an assortment of other medicines and medical supplies (Band-Aids). They did have some creams and ointments for rashes and cuts. Their biggest problem was to determine those inmates that were actually ailing from the inmates trying to get something to try to help them get to sleep at night, or stay awake during the day.

One of the guards would stand next to the nurse at the cart for several reasons. The first was to make sure the inmates lined up in an orderly fashion without incident. There was a red line painted on the floor that the inmates were supposed to stand behind to get their pills. The area was so congested it was hard to form a line. I could barely reach the cart to put my cup down for the nurse to put my pills into it. This was another surprise to me how polite and courteous inmates were in general. Most inmates knew who the really ill inmates were and made sure they got up front and got their meds. As with anything else, things can get screwed up. The nurses didn't always have the medicine right. The guards were usually able to help the nurses, but the guards also rotated. In the event an inmate that needed medicine wasn't being taken care of, the other inmates would step in to help. To any person with common sense and who dealt with inmates for a living, when they recognized loyalty like this taking place, the problem should be resolved quickly and without incident. The problem would be when you would get not-so-smart nurses and guards working at the same time at passing out medicine. I never saw a fight when the nurses came, but I did see innocent inmates who were sticking up for others, trying to help them get their medicine, ending up in 8 hour cell confinement.

Nurses were all female while I was there. Nurses came in all shapes, sizes, races, and attitudes. I found the younger nurses, some in training, were generally the most compassionate. This was probably because they hadn't experienced years of trying to be hoodwinked by inmates trying to abuse the system. These were the inmates who would ruin legitimate needed medical attention for the other inmates. Medication could also be used as trading material. Take some packages of cream I received for a rash that developed on my leg. The nurse was nice enough to give me a six-day supply of the cream. I was to open and rub the cream on my leg, one package each night. I was not the type to trade things with someone that was not in need of help. There was an inmate that was always scratching at his shin—just like I had been. The nurse would not give him anything for the rash. This should have been of concern to all, as staff infection is so prevalent in prisons. This inmate didn't have anything but food to trade for medicine, so he decided he'd just tolerate the itching. My rash cleared up, so I gave him what I had left. He couldn't understand why I just gave it to him. Without knowing it, this became one of the best gestures I ever made there. He stayed polite to me, but a few days later a friend of his came into the POD. Guess what? This new gentleman became my best friend while I was there, and I still write him. Unfortunately he is still in there, and will be for a long time. One just never knows who or what will come of kindness. This became one of my other strongest means of gaining respect, power, and authority in jail.

Oh—there were nurses that would make Nurse Ratchet from *One Flew over the Coocoo's Nest* seem like a Mother Teresa. There was only one nurse that I can use the term, "bitch" to describe. She was mean as hell, and just plain nasty to all of the inmates. She had the mean, scrunched-up face to go with her personality. Inmates aren't stupid. They tolerated her attitude once, because we needed our meds. The next evening not one inmate would go up get to get their medicine. Guards were brought in to take order of the situation. Three of us were made to take our medicine. I was glad to get mine, even though I wasn't going to break ranks with the group. This was a common method used by inmates—you'd have thought Gandhi had taught these men peaceful protest. Too bad more of these inmates didn't apply the same attitude when they were outside of jail. The third night (nurses usually did three consecutive shifts) she wasn't back. In fact, we never saw her again.

Then there was the mandatory water to be taken with any oral medicine. All medicine had to be put into a small paper cup with water. My pills dissolved very quickly, so if one pill got stuck in the cup, it usually was a goner. Because of this stupid rule of putting pills into a cup with water in it I seldom had any idea of how much of a dose of my medicine I was actually taking.

I'll end this part with the lovely thought about the water we were generally forced to use to wash our medicine down. I've mentioned the sole toilet in the common area. Well we either had to hope no one was in the bathroom to get water from the sink in it, or we had to get water from the janitor's closet. I'm not sure which one had the filthiest water. Since most inmates preferred the toilet sink water so did I.

Now for what I thought was one of the biggest jokes of all in this prison, in the nurses' station there was a small-hand written note posted on a window with lots of other signs and notes stuck also. The hand-written note read "$5 CHARGE FOR ALL DOCTOR VISITS." Now I became a pretty regular visitor with my high blood pressure and all.

I never had a doctor check me over. Not once did I see a doctor in the jail. After a while inmates got to know all the nurses, and none were female doctors. There was also a medical form inmates were suppose to fill out to see a nurse or doctor for any ailment. I'd been there a few months and never been billed the $5, and seldom filled the medical-request form out. A lot of inmates were afraid to even ask a nurse for medicine, and there were times where some inmates were really sick. Often they didn't have any money, but usually it was because they would suffer through whatever was ailing them so they could spend the $5 dollars at the commissary. I was able to convince a few inmates that they would not take out the $5. Besides, it would be illegal to charge someone for advice from a nurse. I also found out inmates can be very proud and very stubborn. They didn't want anyone to know they couldn't read or write. I also started to fill out the forms for some of the inmates. About the time I built this trust over not having to pay the $5, sure enough, they started billing inmates the $5 a visit. It was a blessing I was moved to B POD shortly after the other inmates got billed the $5. I still don't think this was a legal fee. How did the prison document and account for taking this $5 from inmates? Where did the money go?

GUARDS

One might have thought that discussing guards would have been one of the first areas I would have discussed. I'm still not sure where I'm going to go with this subject. Like the nurses, they had a hard job. Guards are all different, and handle things and situations differently. Of any subject about my stay, writing about the guards could be the easiest subject to get as ugly, hateful, cruel about, and I wish the worst in life for these folks. Almost as much as I could hope for the police that arrested me. I could go after them verbally. The only thing that would accomplish would be more inner hatred for me to deal with. Believe me; I still struggle with letting this chapter in my life pass, and moving on to a happy, wonderful life. I will say that writing what I have up to this point has been somewhat therapeutic for me, and I don't know where this will end up—but I'm writing it down. My blood pressure actually seems to be remaining relatively calm writing about these folks. I'm not happy for having gone through this experience, especially for what it put my wife, loved ones, family, friends, fellow workers, and all through.

I've mentioned that the guards worked 12-hour shifts. They were all but confined for the duration of this time to a U-shaped console of about a 12-foot-by-12-foot area. The majority of time there was a male and a female guard. I would guess the average age was 40 years old. Many had some military background. We didn't know most of their names or ranks (hard to totally hide, as many had relatives, friends, spouses, etc., in the joint), but for the most part inmates didn't know the guards' names. I'd just get frustrated when some situation would occur and the person asking me the questions would constantly ask which one of the guards or nurses that I had an issue with. It was like you were making the occurrence up because you didn't know guard's or nurse's name. The guards all wore a dark blue, three-button, pullover shirt. The shirts and hats they wore had the insignia of the detention facility. Their khaki pants had lots of pockets. They all wore black, soft-soled shoes. Most of the males shaved their heads or had funky Marine Corps high-and-tight haircut. The women kept their hair cut short or up in a military style. All wore a heavy leather belt with their badges attached. When away from the console they always carried a radio and the keys to the cell doors. They didn't have mace, a knight stick, or any type of weapon on their person. It would be too easy for inmates to attack the guard and get any sort of weapons away from them.

The size of both the males and females varied as much as the normal population of people. There were some that were huge "tall wise," and some that were huge "waist wise." Guards worked 12hour shifts, doing pretty much nothing during those 12 hours except babysit 80 grown men. Who in their right mind would perform such a job? Somebody has to; this work doesn't apply in this case. I don't know how they even try to have some sort of personal life or a family— well, something ain't right with this picture. Not to mention that these officers don't make the best of salaries.

Guards didn't really enforce rules or control the POD most of the time. Inmates, not realizing it, were the ones that made most of the rules and enforced them. One example was the noise. If the majority of the inmates wanted the place quiet it would be quiet. The big problem here was the ignorance of the inmates. The ones usually who bitched and complained the most about the noise generally made the most noise. Fights were usually stopped by other inmates before they got out of control, and any official punishments were handed out because the guards had to. Remember, there were cameras, therefore video tapes of what went on in the entire facility. I talked about the poker playing. Inmates all knew if too many other inmates gathered around a game it was going to be brought to a halt by the guards. The same about inmates gathering around the cells. Inmates regulated other inmates gathering around them. As long as inmates acted rationally, the guards generally left everyone alone.

It was hard to come up with some sort of determination about the personalities of most of the guards, as their job required them to maintain a poker face. There were some guards that once they felt safe and comfortable with you that they would tend to let their guard down, and even treat you like a human being. Then there were some guards that no matter what, they were going to act the way they did, and for most with this characteristic it was a very mean demeanor. There were some that were just plain moody. You had to find out which of their moods they were in before you dealt with them.

My favorite guard was a heavy-set black woman who tried to maintain a positive attitude even when she was reprimanding an inmate. She would take timeout every now and then and just talk to an inmate like he was a regular person. This could backfire on an inmate, as there were a couple of occasions where inmates didn't know if she was kidding or not. One instant was when some heavy gambling began to take place one Saturday afternoon. Several inmates had gathered around the four playing poker. It was a group that usually gambled together. Poker chips were made out of tearing worn-out playing cards into fourths. Color didn't matter. Fifteen chips equaled a bag of some type of snack or food. Twenty chips equaled a candy bar, and 25 chips, a sweet roll. Food on trays, or even entire trays could be gambled for. Side bets could be made by those playing or watching. The card game was determined by the dealer, and I heard some pretty bizarre games made up. This female guard went over and evidently warned them to stop gambling. They thought she was teasing. She wasn't. She finally went to the table and took most of the chips (torn cards) and threw them away. Needless to say there were a good many pissed-off inmates, and their anger was naturally aimed at her. It turned out personnel in C2 had been observing what was taking place on monitors, and everyone knew gambling was going on, but C2 got nervous when too many inmates gathered for most anything. C2 personnel had called down and told her to take the chips and throw them away. Throwing the torn-up cards made the inmates the maddest, as they now had to tear up a better set of cards to make new chips. Things got back to normal after word got out that the guard was not acting on her own.

I served my time in the military when I was young. It was evident that some guards tried to run their shift like the military. What a joke! These guards were not properly trained to be efficient with military-style operations. Again, it was the inmates that maintained most of the way the POD operated. The guards were babysitters. The sergeants were mostly older guards. Inmates didn't like to be treated like they were in the military, and I've mentioned before, they didn't like change. This military mentality did nothing to improve morale or attitudes of inmates in a jail. Being incarcerated was not to be fun, but it was not a place for those in authority to abuse individuals mentally. Inmates are people. Rehabilitation should have been a goal of the penal system for those inmates for whose crime this was appropriate.

Talking small talk can also be a cover-up by the guard. Getting you to start with talking about family and friends can lead to bigger and better information the guard was actually trying to gather. It didn't have to come from just one conversation—it might go on for weeks. Most guards pulled a one-and-one-half-month shift in a POD. Two days on—three days off, and then the opposite. Then the guards usually did something like work the in-processing desk or something, and returned for another shift to the same POD. As I mentioned before, neither the guards nor the inmates liked much change. So here this guard was being buddy-buddy with an inmate for short periods of time, and all of a sudden, a bust of some of this inmate's friends took place. It always amazed me how open and frank so many inmates were to talk about their criminal activities and their friends by name to most anyone. They talked about who their major dealers were and where they lived, who had the money and liked recreational drugs, who was willing to take risks and use weapons. They didn't need stoolies in prison—just put a tape recorder on a guard. Inmates were constantly being moved for their own safety. When I was released I could have told the police who, where, and what drugs were selling. They don't want to know—they already know!

How can I say that? Well, let's look at the common sense of this. Most all prisons are over crowded. So let's say police know where they can bust 20 druggies this coming Friday night at a party. These are just casual users. The police and the system now have a choice. Do we empty out 10 cells, and these 20 inmates, now released prisoners, go in twenty different directions? Or do we allow this drug party to go on without incident, knowing who these druggies are and where they live? The police know they will eventually arrest most of these 20 druggies at the party in the future sometime. The point is, the police prefer to know where the drugs and drug users are located in their jurisdiction. If these drug users wander out of this so-called protected jurisdiction then they become fair game to be arrested. Most are harmless users. Now if there is going to be a major meeting of dealers you better bet the police will be there for that bust! It is a game—a system. With my situation I was out of the system, couldn't get out prison because they didn't know what to do with me. I didn't fit any particular picture.

I have to tell this story—one reason is because it is true. We had a female guard that many of the inmates thought was a "looker." No lie—her fiancé ended up in the POD as an inmate. I'm not sure what for, and it doesn't matter. The two openly flirted around, and it became known throughout the POD that they were engaged. Well, they got caught screwing in the room. I don't know all the facts, but she never came back as a guard in the POD, and he got released shortly thereafter. This is the only sex story I had from my entire stay. Guess you will quit reading now.

Some guards were college educated, for what reason I don't have a clue. Inmate Baby Sitting 101? I have a few college degrees, but I felt the fruits of the accomplishments from the job I went to everyday. What sense of accomplishment these guards got was beyond me.

About the only thing that really stood out to me about the guards was their foul mouths. One would think it would be the inmates doing most of the cursing, but it is the other way around. "GD" is taboo with most inmates. "F-U" is common with some, but it is usually the younger inmates that tend to use the language. "Shit" is the most common curse word used by inmates. GD and F-U were commonly used by the guards. The guards loved to tell inmates very sexually orientated jokes. There were a few times some guards would try to use curse words or provoking statements to bait inmates into some type of conflict. One incident a young, white inmate got upset with a guard. No one ever really figured out what it began over, but within seconds two sergeants were inside the POD in a very aggressive posture and an attitude to go with it. They managed to get the young white inmate upstairs into his cell. In the cell, out of sight and sound pretty much from the general population something took place. The sergeant was allowed to carry a baton, and when we next saw him, he had it out. Now this young inmate wasn't the best model of prisoners, but he wasn't totally stupid either. No one was for sure exactly what went on in the room, but when the sergeant came out he was clearly heard twice saying something about the young man's mother. The second time the young man spit in the sergeant's face. By now there were about 6 officers armed with tazers and batons. That spit landed the kid 90 days in solitary confinement.

INMATES

Where would America be without inmates? If rumors are true our country was founded by released criminals from across the ocean. I don't believe that, but I know people that don't believe 6,000,000 Jews were exterminated either. The point is, do people really know who is being locked up in this country? Or more importantly, do they really care? After my stay I have come to ask myself a number of questions on the subject of prison now that I never would have even thought to ask myself before.

Why is it that America is building all these maximum-security prisons, and who is it they are planning to put into all of these prisons? The general public's picture is murders, rapists, armed robbers, child abusers, and those criminals of some highly violent act. What I found to be the truth is that the majority of those incarcerated are in for "Probation Violation." Say that to yourself three times: probation violation, probation violation, probation violation! Now what does that tell you? If you were like me before—absolutely nothing! Has to be something bad, or they wouldn't be in prison. So when you asked yourself those words, "probation violation" three times were you able to come up with an answer as to what the heck that is? I lived there. I spent 24/7 with these folks. I have an understanding of what the concept is. They either could not afford an outrageous amount that they had to pay a probation officer monthly, pissed dirty or they missed a monthly meeting. The point is, prisons are being built as if every prisoner were an Al Capone, when they are not. The amount of money spent on the amount of security for probation violators is highly unjustified. I've noticed that local politicians who are the advocates for the expenditure of these prisons are not educated as to who they are putting into them. America needs to wake up, as all these high-dollar prisons do is ruin the lives of these individuals. They are needlessly being forced into a lifetime cycle of keeping these prisons full, and that is exactly what the penal system wants and is designed to do. Yes, there are a lot of bad people that need high-security prisons, but someone needs to find out the truth as to what exactly is going on here. I am at least taking the time to write about America's justice system.

I think in layman terms probation was to be a condition for an individual to have a second chance to demonstrate to society that they were capable of abiding by the law. I did pull up a lot of different readings on the subject, and I feel this is a relatively accurate statement. Not legal, but one that can reasonably be agreed upon. A person who has committed a crime and whether or not there is prison time associated, a judge or jury has determined that if a criminal is capable of performing a certain level of performance established by the court then the criminal can return to public life. I know there is a lot more to probation or parole; I'm living it now, but that is the jist of it.

Yes, I ran into what I consider hardened criminals that society should lock up and throw the key away. Most of the hardened criminals that were put amongst us were very scary to live with, as they had nothing to lose if they got in a fight or even killed someone. What they were doing in a POD considered minimal security, mostly pot smokers or people who hadn't paid their bills, or the infamous probation violators, was beyond me. These are not the norm for a correctional detention facility, but there were not enough prisons in America for these types of criminals. And how the term correctional has become associated with a detention facility is also beyond me. If "punishment" is America's term for "correctional," then I guess it fits. Detention Facilities should not be built and run like a penitentiary. The expenses for the amount of security required to build these detention facilities is beyond ridiculous. The treatment and abuses that take place in these detention facilities is not just inhumane, but unnecessary. Some form of rehabilitation is the humane and right way to work with these minimum-security criminals.

It took me over a week to begin to get acclimated as to what was going on in prison. I thought every day I was going to be leaving to go home—and so did some of the other inmates. I wasn't very hungry, so the food-and-snack part didn't come into play with me for some time. I did know what I liked to eat and could eat. Surprisingly I really didn't complain much about the meals until the monotony of the same thing to eat over and over set in. I quickly learned the difference between the two different uniforms being worn in E POD. My dark-blue jump suit meant I was under state jurisdiction, and the blue and white striped jump suits were worn by those under city and county jurisdiction. The POD was split about 50/50 between the two. I also quickly learned wished I was wearing the blue-and-white stripe, as most of these were revolving doors for a few days, a weekend, or a month. The dark-blue could be in the joint for months or even a few years. I was an oddball going home every day, but never leaving. I went from being a good luck charm for inmates to hang out with at first, to being a virtual leper, whom no one wanted to be around. No one understood what was going on with me, especially myself. Like I've said, no one in prison likes anything out of the norm, and I had definitely turned out to be something out of the norm. I didn't even know what the charges were against me. Did I sound like a dummy when another inmate would ask me what I was in for? I'd start making things up to tell them, but then I'd forget who I told what, and that just made things worse. The only thing an inmate hates worse than a child molester is a liar. I also found out several inmates had begun to think I was a plant—a snitch. Things often got really weird for me.

The first day, when I got put in cell 10, there was a young man lying in the top bunk. He was telling me something about what he did (seems like everyone likes to bounce off new arrivals their story to see how good it sounds or where they need to adjust it). He thought he was going to be in there about 3 months, and a few minutes later a guard came to release him. I got his prison-issue supplies and kept the stuff that it was evident he hadn't used.

A little while later another young white boy was brought in. I was still in shock and pain, having been in the place few hours, and now had my second cell mate. Without realizing it I'd already become the occupant of the bottom bunk. The bottom bunk was premium, because one didn't have to climb or jump up and down all of the time. I couldn't with my broken ribs. The other guy wasn't there long enough to tell or show me anything, so my stuff was still pilled on the bottom bunk. Guards don't tell you much of anything unless you piss them off. I hadn't been given the blue plastic matt that is what they called "the mattress." My mind was freaking at how I was going to sleep on this little metal bunk with a tiny sheet and blanket. I was also wondering things like, *Where are my pajamas? How am I going to call my wife and tell her good night? Figure out schedules to do things, as there are no clocks? Only the guards wear watches. When will we eat? Where are we going to eat?* My mind was going crazy, as this was during a lock-down, and when the doors opened I was afraid to even wander out of the cell. Then the new cell mate had freaked out while we were still locked in our cells. I wanted to do the same, but was too afraid to. He began crying until he was going into convulsions. I knew what an intercom was and pushed the button inside the cell. I told the voice at the other end what was going on. Soon some guards came into the room and dragged the young boy out of the place, never to be seen again. A guard finally brought me a blue mattress and told me to make my bunk.

I put the sheet and blanket on as well as they would fit. No one knows or cares how a bunk is made as long as the sheet and blanket are not just wadded up on the bunk. I came to learn the punishment for leaving one's bed unkempt was usually a 4-hour confinement in one's cell. Never happened to me. In fact I was never placed on any type of punishment the entire stay. Not a model prisoner—just never liked to be punished for any reason my entire life—but here I was in jail.

So I lost my second cell mate in a matter of hours. I began to think this was normal until later that afternoon I received my third cell mate of the day. Oh yeah—I also kept all the toiletries the second cell mate left. This time all was usable, as he wasn't there long enough to use anything. What I am talking about when I mention toiletries? It was a very small glad bag with a funky zip-lock top. Inside were a few items: a comb, a one-inch toothbrush, enough of a tube of toothpaste for two, maybe three days, a bottle of shampoo, and small hotel-complimentary-sized wrapped soap. That was it. Remember, one can buy all of the Bob Barker items at the commissary, but you really pay a price, and the toothpaste is not Crest either.

By now it was after lunch, and I'm not sure if I ate anything, but we were back in lock-down when my cell door was opened once again. I had another cell mate. This time it was a young black male with corn rows. He had his prison face on, and merely made his way to the top bunk without fuss. I say this because I later learned the bottom bunk was the bunk of choice, and there were physical fights over who got to sleep on bottom. So what was so special about being on the bottom bunk? Well, first, you didn't have to climb up to get in, and most jumped down to the concrete floor to get down. This was critical when one was all but asleep and woke up needing to piss. Second, the one on the bottom bunk was much more mobile without disturbing the other. This became critical for me when I started spending much of the night writing my wife letters. Besides, at 52 and with my bum leg from the police pounding my knee with their heavy-duty flashlights, I couldn't manage to even get up into the top bunk. Later I will tell about my experience of sleeping on the cold concrete floor, because I was placed into a cell where the inmate already had the bottom bunk. Trying to get up and down also got my blood pressure going pretty heavy. No sympathy from the guards on that matter. Had to have a profile from the medical staff to be assigned a bottom bunk permanently, and high blood pressure didn't qualify for such a profile. Poor me!

So now I had a new cell mate, and I don't think we talked for three or so days. He seemed nice enough, just didn't talk much. Not even to the other brothers in the POD. He was a good-sized young man and spent of good bit of time doing crunches and push-ups. Crunches are where you find most anything able to hold your weight and with pure arm strength push yourself up and down. Pretty much like doing pushups. There were numerous styles of working out without the weights in the prison. I wasn't into any of the body building. I just wanted to get the hell out of the place, and in one piece.

This new cell mate ended up being a major blessing for me. He was a local dude, and this place was nothing new to him. After a few days he opened up and started talking a little to me. The first time he talked to me I will never forget as he started by laughing at me. I hadn't noticed there was the small lump in the mattress for a pillow. I had been sleeping with it at my feet and upside down. Though putting the mattress the right way didn't do much good for my sleep it had opened some dialog between us. He still wasn't much of a talker, and was in for probation violation—pissed dirty. I didn't know it until later, but all he had to do was pay a little over $100 to walk. He was young but had a lot of good philosophy and perspectives in life for his age. I'd generally listen to him talk and wonder why he didn't try to practice more of what he thought. I learned a few other things about prison life and surviving being in the joint. He wasn't too prejudiced, but we stayed away from any such topics. His refusal to pay the $100 bond to get out that he was protesting was thwarted by a terrible toothache. He paced the room for three or four nights without getting anything more than aspirin from the nurses and the usual lip service about seeing a dentist soon. He was there all of 7 days, and never had to spend an hour in the place. And here I was, still leaving every day— or so I still thought. The day he left he'd just been to the commissary and filled his Tupperware box with toiletries and other items. I was sure he was going to give them to a brother inmate, but he gave most everything to me. My first pair of socks—I was in heaven, as my family still didn't know all that was going on with me and how the system worked money wise.

This time I didn't get a new cell mate right away. Getting a new cell mate came in an unusual way. There was a young kid that was another probation violator for drugs. I'd met him before in the common area but didn't particularly care for him—turned out I didn't really like his then cell mate. Well, he couldn't get along with his older, white, Bull Shit-artist cell mate. Things finally came to a head between them, and he told a guard if he wasn't moved to another cell something was going to happen. I heard the conversation and didn't think much of it. It didn't dawn on me about not having a cell mate at the time, and the place stayed full. The guard surprised me by coming over to talk to me. He asked if it would be okay for the young white male to move into my cell? This was a first. A guard asking an inmate permission to do something wasn't too common. They usually barked out orders, and he was asking me, of all people. I said, sure, he could move in, as at least I knew the type inmate I was getting for a cell mate. One of the biggest fears, it turns out, in jail, is when you lose a cell mate what type of new one are you going to get? Turned out this was going to be a long period for two cell mates to stay together, as his sentence was 90 days for his probation violation. A rather long time, but it wasn't his first offense. I was leaving tomorrow, but it turned out he left before me by a long time.

Surprising to me, we hit it off right away. He'd just been unhappy with the other jerk he had for a cell mate. In all the time we were there together we never argued once. He was happy with the upper bunk, and my writing my wife at night didn't bother him. I'd learned from my previous cell mate that another key to success of getting along was not to spend too much time together during the day, as nights could get long and the days could too. He had his clique of friends, as he, too, was a local boy and knew other inmates. I just tended to get along with most everyone, so I always felt like there was someone I could visit or whatever with. My days went slowly, but my new cell mate and I had a ball after lock-down at night. We would keep each other up for a while laughing our asses off, usually just acting stupid. He didn't know what to think of this goofy old man, as most inmates thought I was a quiet, reserved individual. I'd put on a silly show at night for him.

We also became protective of one another. On more than one occasion his youth and ignorance in general would piss off an inmate, and I would step in to calm things down. He did the same for me, as no matter how good one is to the other inmates, even being good can piss an inmate off. Most anything can set off an inmate—that is why it is so stressful 24/7 in prison. One is always just one step away from being punched out.

I'll call him Charlie, as he did become my angel in many respects, and certainly helped me survive my time while he was there. Charlie taught me how to play Casino. That lasted for all of two nights, as I started beating him. I would joke and try to dance around the cell with my bum knee just to make him laugh. It usually worked. Charlie was the type that if there was a fight or something to break out he would have to be right there in the middle of what was going on. I, on the other hand, would run for the safety of cell, locking the door behind me. He thought that was just too funny. After he learned I did this he would always ask me, if some scuffle broke out, whether I ran to the cell to lock myself in to be safe. I always did. He even found me one time hiding in the corner of the cell with my blanket over my head so no one could find me.

Being in a place 24/7 there were times we did things together. I just thought of the time I thought I was dying from eating the chocolate. I keep buzzing the guard, but they were ignoring me. He finally told me to tell them I thought I was dying, and the guard finally sent me to see the nurse. Charlie was prison smart—sort of. He scared me sometimes with things he would say to other inmates without thinking. He was lucky most just took him as being young and dumb, and ignored him.

Then the strangest thing happened to Charlie and me. A guard woke us up—it must have been about 4 a.m. or so. My first thought was, I was finally going home. Then the guard told us both to pack our stuff; we were moving. I still wasn't sure what was going on— moving? Why would they want to move us both at the same time? Did the guards think we were having too much fun being cell mates? I was half asleep and hardly moving. Charlie seemed to know what was going on and not telling me anything for some reason. He was almost all packed, when I'd just started. He still hadn't said a word to me. I then began to think I was the one being moved to another cell, and he'd gotten an early release. It happens that when they want to make room for new inmates, especially if they are still gigged up, they want them to sleep it off in a cell by themselves. Inmates still gigged up can get very violent and hurt themselves badly. Usually if they are still that messed up they strap them down on a Gurney and put them in isolation until they come down off the drugs they're on. I was stunned and in a state of shock, as I couldn't figure out what was going on. All packed, we both walked up to the guard's console. It was then I found out we were being moved to a different POD. I'd never heard of such a thing unless an inmate was being punished and being sent to a higher-security POD. The guard finally told us we were being transferred to B POD. I'd never heard of B POD. I'd heard of PODs D, F, G, and H—but never B POD. Oh yeah—A POD was where the woman were kept. B POD was for all the state prisoners, and we all wore the dark-blue jump suits.

HOME—B POD

The guard in E POD opened the door to the hallway, and I just followed Charlie out, walking behind him down the hallway. It wasn't far before he stopped at a door with a glass window, indicating it was a POD. Sure enough there was a sign B POD. C2 opened the outer door, and we walked in. There was a female guard standing at the new console who opened the door into the B POD for us. She greeted us and told us we had two choices for what were to become our new cells. Charlie picked the one up stairs to the right, and I was left with the one up stairs to the left.

Needless to say I was scared, but even more, I was sad that Charlie and I were being separated, even though we were still in the same POD together.

Things changed quickly. Charlie became sort of a smart ass, as he only had 7 days left, and he would let everyone in the new POD know it—constantly. He got so bad about talking about leaving I eventually had to separate myself from him for my own safety. I had still set my goal on leaving the same day as Charlie, but even that soon faded. I just wanted to go home.

The next day I found out what the move from E POD to B POD was all about. The first thing that stood out was that everyone in this new POD was wearing the dark-blue jump suits. Turned out I was now with all inmates under state supervision. State inmates generally stayed a minimum of 30 days, as that was how often state court or superior court convened. The city and county courts met twice weekly, and the inmates in the blue-and-white-striped jump suits, as I've mentioned, were the revolving-door inmates. I'd been left in E POD so long because the system never really knew what to do with me. Now someone decided to put me with all of the other state inmates. I had to re-establish myself all over again. It hadn't been that easy to do in E POD, as inmates didn't stay long enough usually to even get to know them. Respect came from size, power, and money. I would come to learn that B POD was greatly different in many ways.

Things didn't start off too swiftly for me in my new POD. The first thing was that in my haste to pack, and not knowing why, I'd left my hospital blanket behind. Hospital blankets were larger and warmer. Fortunately the guard was understanding and called to inform E POD I was coming back to get my blanket. I no sooner got back to my new cell when I noticed I'd also left my towel behind. There was no way I was going to ask to go back for it. Hell—I'd dry off with my wash rag if I had to. I did manage to get a new towel the next day.

The first thing I noticed was how much quieter it was in this new POD. Turns out that when folks or inmates stay longer in a place they are able to take more control over what goes on. It also appeared that the majority of the inmates were older, which also made a difference.

All of these factors, and others, resulted in an entirely different style of living in this POD. Inmates were around long enough to develop relationships or decide not to develop relationships. Most knew how long they were going to be staying, and how long the other inmates would be around. I was still leaving every day, but didn't say anything to anyone.

The days seemed to pass quicker, maybe because the nights didn't seem so endless with the noise now ending at 10 p.m. lock-down. I actually had a little trouble getting used to the quiet. The constant, loud ringing in my ears quieted down a good bit. I wasn't as anxious as I had constantly stayed before. My sense of urgency to be ready for something violent to happen at any given moment went away. I began to relax some.

The food was the same. The same nurses brought around the medicine. There were some slight differences in the way linen exchange, personal clothes washing, and other general activities were handled. One could both watch and hear the TVs. I didn't care for Texas Walker, CSI, and most of the other shows always on the TVs.

The next few days flew by, and in no time it was Charlie's day to leave. Didn't turn out as emotional as it would have been if we'd stayed put in E POD, but I was still happy for him to be leaving. Never have heard from him again, but that is the norm for inmates. Intentions are good about staying in touch, but the reality is that it best to just say good-bye and move on in life.

My new cell mate had the bottom bunk, and from the sound of it he was going to be staying for a while. It took me a while but I managed to get up on the top bunk one time. I hated it. Not because it was higher, just the fact I knew it would be a major pain in the butt getting up and down all the time, plus the pain of my ribs. Then I decided to try to get down, and that proved even more difficult than getting up. It was right then I decided I'd be putting my mattress on the concrete floor and sleeping there.

My new cell mate was strange. He was about my age and had spent a good bit of his life in prison. He'd been brought from another state for another trial. He lied all of the time so I hated to even talk to him. He had so many different stories as to why he was in the jail that I don't think he even knew the reason. Then I found out he was actually a jail-house snitch. He'd been transported from another prison to specifically gather information on some inmates in the POD. I know this for a fact! For some reason the jerk let me read the official documents he had detailing for him what his instructions were for the deal he'd agreed to.

It was less than an hour after he'd let me read all that crap about his situation that my luck changed for the good once again. He was an avid reader, and had money to buy plenty of snacks. Books were often hard to come by, and he would horde 4 or 5 books at a time. Inmates were supposed to read and pass on books. He'd also use books for trading material. He would want snacks from an inmate for a book.

This was unacceptable. Anyway, he'd come in the room and gathered up the 5 or so books he had to take down to the Thursday book cart to exchange them. He also ended up with a document in his hand, but when he turned to return to the cell and put the document away the cell door somehow locked. I was lying on the floor when he began to frantically bang on the window, as though I could let him in. He finally put the papers under the door, and pointed for me to put them in his box. He then headed back downstairs. I was putting the papers in his box, as there was no way I was going to read anymore of his stuff. I heard the door unlock about this time. As I walked to the door I heard a loud noise like a slap, and looked out just in time to see his feet fly up in the air and him land hitting his head on the concrete floor. He was clearly out cold. I'd just been in the POD a week now and was just getting to know some of the inmates. I recognized the tall black older gentleman who had just laid my cell mate out. There were also the 5 books scattered about, and as most books were worn out, they were in pieces.

I was somewhat amazed that the guards had little reaction to what happened. They had my cell mate carried out. The guards did calmly escort the man that had hit him into the multi-purpose room where he waited for the sergeant to come and evidently get his story.

There were two stories that quickly floated about the POD and got back to me. One sounded like a cover up. This story was that the punch was thrown because he had been taking snacks from the other inmates for the books he was hoarding. I would have believed that, as inmates take books and reading very seriously. But the second story made more sense and scared the hell out me. It had been found out that he was a snitch, and that was the reason for the punch. The rumor went further to include me as being a snitch as well. Not many inmates knew I'd been transferred from E POD and had been in the jail for a couple months already. I wasn't some new arrival, nor was I a planted snitch.

There was some retaliation directed towards me later that afternoon. Strangely I was called to the nurse's station to get my blood pressure checked. The POD was in lock-down when I left, as there is always a lock-down after all violent events. When I returned the inmates were out of their cells, and my door was wide open. Now I didn't have a cell mate, as he was either in the nurse's station or at the hospital for the beating he took.

I went into my cell. There was my box, out in the middle of the room with the lid off. I looked inside and saw that all of my under clothing appeared to be in place. But—all of my snacks were gone. I'd just been to the commissary, and even though I don't buy a lot of junk to eat, I was pissed off that my stuff had been stolen. And even worse, it seemed the guards were a part of what had taken place by not watching the cell at all while I was out. The door to my cell wasn't even supposed to be opened with me out of the POD.

So what was lucky about all of this happening? Well, I did have some food stolen, but the bottom bunk was back to being mine. No more sleeping on the concrete floor, or so I hoped. I still had no idea how much longer I was going to be in this jail.

My blood pressure started to get the best of me after this all happened. I just plain didn't feel good anymore. I finally had enough and demanded to go to the nurse's station. I told them I wanted to withdraw my waiver and get my blood pressure medicine 4 times a day as my doctor prescribed. Fortunately for me there was a good nurse working. She took me to one of the offices and we just began to talk. She told me how bad being in solitary confinement was, that it was not just the isolation, boredom, and other things most people associate with being all alone. It was the fact that so many inmates literally lost their minds, and never recovered from what they experienced from being in solitary confinement. Some were now mentally retarded for life. Many have constant thoughts of committing suicide. I could relate to when I was first put in a cell and had the crazy idea of ramming my head into the wall. Needless to say, when we were finished talking I was going back to a B POD once again.

I did have a nervous breakdown while I was first in this new POD. My blood pressure got so bad that I couldn't stop shaking. It started in my hands and proceeded to extend to my entire body. I was barely able to fill out a medical form. I didn't know if I was having a stroke or what. All I did know was that no one cared what was happening to me. The bitch of a guard called me a crybaby, no nurse would come to the POD, and I was not allowed to go to the nurse's station. I was told all that could be done was for me was to go lie down until it passed. Hell—it could have been nothing more than a panic attack that I couldn't explain that brought it on, but it did pass. One thing I learned is that if you die in prison no one cares. When I say no one cares, I'm referring to the prison employees. I know my wife, family, and friends would all care deeply. I also learned you are on your own in prison, and if you are going to survive for however long, it is all up to you and your faith in the Lord.

Even in prison God is there to look out for you, and I can't count the number of times he saved me in more ways than my health. I'll have plenty more on this, I promise, because, as I've said before— Jailhouse Religion is for real and very powerful. I've used the term, "lucky" from time to time—it means I was lucky to have God on my side.

It was a day or so later I came across the gentleman I still consider my best friend during my incarceration. Since I've used Charlie I think I will call him Charles. He came at a time when I really needed someone who cared. Charles was a black man, about my age, white hair and very fit looking—a very distinguished individual.

I'm still thankful to the other inmate that had introduced me to Charles. Charles and I didn't do a whole lot together except spend time talking. Charles was a very gracious, caring, and sharing individual. He could take care of himself if needed, but over the years had learned to control his temper. Unfortunately he too liked to smoke weed a bit, and just didn't have any luck with the law.

JAIL

I know how our relationship evolved. It was from what became known as the senior citizens' table. There were four of us, and out of respect, our table remained reserved for all of us for most every meal. Occasionally a new inmate would come and sit at the table without knowing he had moved into our territory. We all took care of each other to make sure no one went hungry. So did the younger inmates— made sure we were all taken care of. This wasn't just food either. We'd make sure all knew when the nurses were there with our medicines, and again, younger inmates would help ensure we were taken care of. This respect continued until the day I was finally released. I have written Charles once, but I'm sure it is the last we will have any contact with each other.

SHAKE DOWNS

One of the pleasures was enduring a shake down of the POD. I'll never forget my first. The shake down started shortly after 10 p.m. lock-down, when all of the inmates were safely locked away in their cells. There was a strange commotion and noises going on outside in the common area. I was on my bunk writing my wife a letter, as usual. I got up to look out. My cell mate Charlie said there were probably 6 guards with rubber gloves and plastic bags with them. Sure enough, that was exactly what I saw. He told me a shakedown was about to take place. That these guards were going to be going through each of the cells. That each of us would have to be strip searched first, and then wait outside the cell while they rummaged through every cell. They were looking for contraband. Contraband was anything that an inmate wasn't supposed to have in the cell. If they found anything they would confiscate it. They were looking for cigarettes, marijuana, cocaine, or any other illegal substance they could get their hands on.

The guards on our floor finally came into our cell. One told me to strip first, so I did. Then he told me to put my hands up against the wall and lean forward. It was then I heard him pop his glove on his wrist. I got braced for what was coming next when he told me to spread my legs further apart. Memories of getting a physical to join the military flashed in my mind. Damn, this guy is really going to get me good. I could already feel his cold glove up my ass. He then told me to cough hard twice. I wasn't sure what that was all about, unless coughing helped relax the muscles or something. Turned out that was all there was to the strip-search part. They just wanted to see if any contraband was stuck up your ass.

JAILHOUSE RELIGION

My family is Methodist and has always been very involved in church activities. I was to until I hit high school. Unfortunately, I let the school extracurricular activities take over my attending church and church activities. Over the years I've been to church occasionally, and always felt good going—wondering why I could just never make going a full-time part of my life.

The first several weeks I was in prison I would do like most inmates, by sitting outside the religious activities looking in. There was a one-hour church service on Sunday. On Monday a missionary would visit and share things he had accomplished or done over the years. On Thursday a deacon from a local church would come. Every evening there was prayer call, where inmates would come into the multipurpose room, form a circle holding hands, and each would say a prayer out loud (if they wanted to, and most all did).

One evening I was sitting outside the multi-purpose room when the call went out for prayer call. Sitting in my chair, bored as usual, something compelled me to get up off my butt and go in. I wasn't sure what was going to take place, and to be honest, I almost let my fear get me to walk right back out of the room. I stayed, and thank God I did.

There were about 10 of the 80 inmates in attendance. Anyone in the group can start with their prayer, and the prayers would continue around the entire circle. Sometimes there were special requests or short talks about anything a person wanted to talk about.

During the other 3 services, time was of the essence, as only one hour was allowed, so the guests, who were all dynamic, would do almost all of the talking. Each of the three different services, left all the inmates full of hope, cheer, and forgiveness.

The church service was conducted by a gentleman who had been shot and stabbed several times. The missionary had traveled the world and spent time with some very incredible individuals. The deacon was a man with a vision that inspired the entire group.

I began to attend all 3 services and the prayer group every evening. I experienced things I cannot explain, but there was definitely power in that room. I witnessed some of the roughest young men converted, many others renew their relationship with God, and the love and caring that took place was overwhelming. For the first time in my life I actually experienced and now understand the Holly Ghost—the carrier of the message. My last evening I had a lot delivered to me from God, but two events I will share. Our group had amassed about 20 out of 80 inmates attending regularly. My last evening was not supposed to happen, as I went before the judge the day before, but due to a technicality I was held over a day. Something told me it was for a reason, and I stayed calm the entire next day and on into the evening, even past lock-down. God kept telling me there was a reason. Well, that evening the gentleman had been saying one of us was going to leave that week—God keep telling me it was me. That evening, I almost wasn't there for what became my last prayer call. I was placed in the center of the group, and they performed a laying of hands on me. I'd never witnessed this before, but the last visit I had with my lawyer I told him to look up Timothy 4:14. This was days before the event happened.

"Neglect not the gift that is in thee, which was   given thee by prophecy, with the laying on of the hands of the presbytery."

I remembered that verse from my youth. It happened, and it happened to me. The second occurrence was after the 10 p.m. lock-down. God was still keeping me calm. I was packed, as I just knew I was going to be leaving shortly that evening, not the next day. It was probably about 10:15 when my name was called out. With great joy I gathered my belongs, heard the lock on the door open, and walked out. To my shock and dismay there were heads and hands clapping in every cell I looked into. I didn't know all of these men, but I knew God was there with all of us. When I got to the guards' console with my stuff I could see the dismay in the eyes of both guards. They weren't sure what was going on.

Some 70 or more men standing at their windows to their cells clapping, chanting, and cheering my name. I heard a voice from C2 come over the console speaker asking the guards what the heck was going on. One guard responded with, "I don't know sir, I've never seen anything like this before." The other guard had heard my name amongst all the cheering. She looked into my eyes and said, "This is for you, isn't it?" I shrugged my shoulders and walked out to the door to wait for C2 to open my way into the hallway for the very last time. I did look back once. I looked up into Charles' cell, he was standing there, and we waved to each other. I was out.

ATTORNEYS

I've had to really think about how to address this subject. I've tried to keep everything I've written as objective and positive as possible. Attorneys are a very sore subject with me, but I don't want my total disgust for them affect what I've tried to achieve in writing about my experience. Here is what I will do—continue to write as objectively about my experience (again this is not about my case), and let the cards fall as they may.

I had two types of attorneys. The first was a public defender, and the second was a hired criminal lawyer. In the beginning it was just my wife and me trying to figure out what was going on and how to proceed. We had absolutely no money, so we found out after I'd been in the place a few days that I qualified for a public defender, our being indigent.

I'd been in prison a few days, was still in shock and pain, when a guard called me and told me I was to go to in-take. At this time I hadn't been out of the POD for anything, and now I found myself out in the empty hallway with no idea where I was going or what I was doing. This is not good. After wondering about for a bit I heard a voice come over the hallway intercom asking me what I was doing. Not sure which end of the hall the guard was talking from, as there was a C2 at each end, I just shrugged my shoulders. Evidently the person called the guard in the POD and asked them where and what I was doing. I once again heard the voice. I was given directions as to where I was going. So I got to in-take. The guard there asked my name and what I was there for. Once again I felt about stupid as hell, as I still really didn't know where I was, or what I was there for. The guard called back to the POD and found out I was there to talk to the woman that gathers information to determine first, if you want a lawyer, second, if you want a public defender or a paid lawyer. I told her I had no money, so I guessed I wanted a public defender. She then proceeded to ask me questions. I finally figured out this was to determine if I qualified for a public defender at taxpayers' expense. A couple of days went by, and I was again sent back to intake. This time I knew to ask the POD guard questions like where I was going and why was I going there.

I got to in-take, and after a good, long wait, a nice-looking black lady called me into the small office room. She presented her as being appointed as my public defender. She opened her briefcase, taking out a form she would fill out with information about me, and I thought, about my case. She proceeded to ask me questions. Most were yes/no type questions, but others were about details of my case. She would want a yes/no answer, and it quickly became apparent she was not there to treat me like a client. She was there to get in get answers as quickly as possible, and move on to the next inmate. The waiting room was full—20 or so inmates. I realized that I was screwed, as I didn't get a chance to explain anything about what had happened, and I was out of the room headed back to the POD. I was told it would be 2 more weeks or more before I would go before the judge—no jury.

For 2 weeks I had to put up with listening to jailhouse judges—the inmates. Some would tell me, "Nothing to it"—I'd walk. That I might even get out before without even going to court, as the holidays were upon us, and the prison was packed. It was true; inmates were being released early, but they were all city or county inmates. No one wearing the state dark-blue jump suits left early. Others would tell me I was going to be put away for a long time. My mind was fried. I didn't know what to think, and was tired of even trying to make sense out of my even being in there, let alone a trial.

It seemed like an eternity, but my 2 weeks passed, and I was called, along with others, being told we were going to court. We were then escorted out to the hallway and taken to a new room with holding cells. During the holidays prisons get overfilled with inmates, so there was nowhere to sit in the holding cell. It got hot, and I didn't know what was going on. There were so many of us we over flowed into another holding-cell room. After a long wait they began taking inmates out a few at a time. I could finally see out the window, and we were all getting hand, waist, and leg shackles put on. We were going to wear our jump suits to go into court. Mine was all torn up. The snaps at my crouch didn't stay shut, and I had no underwear on. We would walk into court wearing our Bob Barker flip flops, and I didn't even have socks.

It took a good while to get us all shackled, and then a guard began to lead us in single file to the court. The court was in a room that was across the street, so I got the privilege of walking under in what was called "The Grey Tunnel." It seemed like forever. We finally got there, and all of us were placed into a single holding cell. Once again there was nowhere to sit down. I noticed that my toes were bleeding from the long walk and the flip flops rubbing them. This was so inhumane, I can't describe how I felt.

The room quickly became hot, and the loud noise persisted. I thought I was going to lose my mind for real, and here I was about to go before a judge. Many of the inmates had been through this process before, so they were the ones who were know-it-alls about everything. Once again I was being told every conceivable thing that could happen in my case. I just keep praying. God was always there to get me through the worst of times. This was really bad. I almost passed out from the heat, weakness of my body, and my mind spinning and getting dizzy. After a good while guards started opening the door and calling out names. Slowly inmates were leaving the room. I thought, *Good,* at first, but then they started coming back. They'd been before the judge. Some were excited at the good news they got, and some came back mad. I saw one so mad he punched the concrete wall, and I know he broke his hand. The room became hotter, louder, and now much more intense.

It seemed like hours before my name was finally called. I made my way outside the cell door and saw a sea of men and women dressed in suits. One grabbed me, and the next thing I knew I was in a courtroom, standing before a judge. I felt totally naked inside my filthy jump suit, was wearing shackles, and my feet were bleeding as I was standing in a courtroom. Then I had a gentleman standing next to me. My mind was spinning—I was supposed to have a female lawyer, not this total stranger.

I didn't even have time to look around before this strange man next to me told to sit down, and he began talking to the judge. I didn't even know his name. First thing, he couldn't even get my name right. Then he said I'd worked a few years for the company I was with. I'd worked there 30 years, since I was 17 years old, consecutively with this company (with the exception of a few years of going to college). I tried to tell him that, but he told me, "Shut-up!" In fact all he ever told me was, "Stand-up, "Sit-down," "Shut-up." He didn't know a thing about me and didn't present any type of defense for me. The next thing I knew the district attorney started talking. This man was loaded for bear against me. Everything out of his mouth was a lie, and my public defender didn't say anything except to tell me to "Shut up!" I got dizzy and felt like my legs were going to collapse out from under me. I don't remember much more other than being led out of the courtroom. I can't even tell you what the judge looked like. This public defender's last words to me were, "Get me more information for your appeal," and I was back in the holding cell. I was mad as hell at the total lack of defense I was provided. I wanted to cry because I knew I'd be going back to the POD for a good while, and I wanted my wife so badly. This entire process had started at 8 a.m. and I got back to the POD after 3 p.m. Oh, they had saved my meal tray from lunch and were just starting to serve dinner—real yummy!

My family finally got involved, and to make a long story a little shorter, they hired me a paid lawyer.

The district attorney went first, and again he was loaded for bear— only a grizzly bear this time. Everything out his mouth was either a total distortion of the facts or outright lies. My lawyer didn't object to anything. How could he? He didn't know anything. This continued for a while until the District Attorney.

Thank God my family came through for me and hired me an excellent attorney. Now I don't know for sure how good the Public Defender is, but I know I'm not spending any time in prison because of my new lawyer. Praise the Lord!

COURTS

Not all courts are like the ones shown on TV. Most are not OJ Simpson trials. I stood about 8 feet in front of the judge. He had a little throne he sat in, nothing special. The two attorneys stood on each side of me. There probably was room for a jury in the room, if there was a jury trial. There were ladies and gentlemen with computer monitors they peered over while I was in there. The judge started the proceeding. There was no swearing in. The lawyers would say their thing, and it was over. I've still never had the chance to tell my side of what occurred.

The police were trying to nail me good by never telling what all of my charges were at one time. At this initial hearing the judge read 6 charges were filled by the police against me. At one time my lawyer told me it was up to 15 charges. This really messed with my mind. My lawyer managed to get me out from going to jail.

This isn't an every day event for most folks, so most don't know how the system operates other than what people have seen on TV. It is all very scary. There are no such things as rights. The only rights a person has seems to depend on how much money one has in his back pocket.

RESPECT AND SURVIVING

I mentioned that I would talk some about how I was able to obtain the respect that is essential for surviving in prison. By surviving I am talking about life-and-death situations that can and do happen in jail. I was worried about coming out with all of my teeth, no broken bones, and the like. I had to learn prison life quickly.

I've already mentioned a few of the things that brought me the respect that an inmate needs, if for no other reason, just to make life a little more enjoyable or bearable.

My being older was probably the major factor in gaining respect. It really isn't the being older, but the being wiser. There were grumpy old men in there that no one would give the time of day. I tended to be quiet, modest, and pretty much let my actions speak the loudest for me. I learned quickly that what might sound to be the smartest advice or philosophy on a subject today might, the very next day, be the worst thing you could have ever said. Like when I helped some inmates fill out the medical form. It wasn't worth arguing any subject, because nobody is right in prison, but at the same time nobody is wrong. This is not the place a person wants to settle a disagreement by ending up in a fight. That just gets you time in solitary—still guys would come to blows over the stupidest of arguments.

With my age also came my illness of having high blood pressure and the need for medicine. Once inmates get to know you and develop even a little bond they can become very protective of you. In all the time I was in there I only missed pill call a few times. Inmates of all ages, races, whatever, would go out of their way to find me to make sure I got my meds. I was surprised how many of the younger inmates really understood about how important it is for one to get their blood-pressure medicine till I learned many of them had a close relative who either took blood pressure medicine or had even passed away from high blood pressure. Even as small as the place sounds to be, a person can go missing for a time. I was usually in the shower in the evening, which was where they would find me for pill call. Other places I'd be were napping or whatever in my cell. A few times I was out shooting the basketball. There were a couple times the nurse came during one of our religious services. Not only did I feel bad if I had to go another 12 hours without my medicine, but I could have died.

Being able to shoot a basketball and to shoot one really well, especially for my age, was the first time I actually noticed respect inside jail. In the beginning I would go out shooting around. One day I came in, and a number of inmates came up to me and mentioned something like "Hey Old man, you're a pretty good basketball player." I will say that for some reason, I know it came from above, I couldn't seem to miss on that goal. I should say goals, as my ability to make baskets continued over into B POD as well. There were even young black inmates that could play some ball who would ask me advice on their shot or something like that. I could play the games like Around the World or at the most 21, but when it came to a real game of 3 on 3, I'd have to step aside. The Bob Barker flip flops weren't the reason I wouldn't play—I just didn't want to get hurt!

Inmates are proud people, just like most people are, and like the stories about the education level of prisoners is true. I found many could not read or write. They didn't want anyone to know this about them. I would be a little amazed at the penmanship of so many individuals when it came to signing their name, and then I'd learn that writing their name was about all they could write. Over time inmates found out I was willing to help with filling out forms, like the medical request form, write short letters, and even help to the best of my ability with writing some legal letters. But more important was the fact that they learned I would not go around telling others. I was very proud of the fact that in working with a couple inmates on their legal problems, I was actually able to get them an early release, or some of the conditions that the judge originally ordered were dismissed.

Inmates quickly learned who had the money to buy snacks at the commissary—hell, it was evident when a dude would come back with two or three grocery bags full of snacks. Most knew I had a little money, but spent it on pens, paper, stamps, and envelopes. Snacks were not a priority with me. I usually would get something out to munch on after evening lock-down while I was writing my letters. It wasn't to horde the little food I had—it just became my routine. Now there were times I would bring a snack out to eat while watching TV or whatever. Inmates would become like vultures, and all of a sudden they'd act like they were your best friend to get you to share your food. Then they'd act like they were your worst enemy when it became evident to them you weren't going to share with them. I shared with those inmates I chose to share with. Sharing food was a strange thing, too. When you think about sharing say chips, the person would put their hand out and you would pour a few chips into it. Most of the time when this process would take place the one giving the food would give the other inmate more than half of what was in the already fairly small package of food. Same thing with a candy bar. You didn't just break off a little piece to share. It was usually half or more of the candy bar.

THOUGHTS IN GENERAL

Just like life in general, there is good and bad in everything. Now it's easy to sit back and condemn, curse, hate, blame, and any and everything evil to describe prison. Most of what I have written has been of the negative things about my experience in prison. Prison is not designed to be a vacation resort—it is to serve a purpose in society. The primary purpose is to protect society. The term, "society," means people, property, rights, animals, the environment, and the world in general. Those that cannot abide by what has been determined to be safe for the world have decided on life in prison. The American judicial system is generally viewed as fair. This system is based on right and wrong. There are no grey areas in right and wrong. The grey areas are in the minds of people, and that is the reason for the need of a judicial system.

Grey areas in the minds of people are the reason systems' rules, laws, prisons, judicial methods, punishments, and all else vary from city to city, county to county, state to state, and even amongst the nine Supreme Court Justices. Different regions around America have different moral views, and different beliefs. Look at California and the Gay Marriage law.

There was a young black man, I'd say about 22 years old. He was pretty buffed, like most of the inmates were. The first time I saw him he was on the PAY TEL phone just banging and cussing it. I was told he was trouble, and this wasn't his first time in the place. He also knew some of the other young inmates that were also trouble makers. I just stayed away from him, as he wanted to argue with everyone, including the guards. I'd been going to the religious services and nightly prayer call for a while at the time. One day he showed up to the Sunday service. The meanness, the violence in his face and body language was gone. He looked content. Most of us who attended regularly had Bibles or would share them. The guest speakers would often reference a scripture and ask us to turn to the page—it was good practice or often refreshed my memory. Some guests brought highlighters so we could mark certain verses. I still have my Bible and have been amazed at how often our preacher is using the verses I marked while in jail. Anyways, this young man seemed interested in looking into the words of a Bible, something told me, but no one was sharing a Bible with him. After a while I got up and went across the room and gave him my Bible to use for the rest of the service. Most of the inmates that came to any of the services were black, as that was the race of most of the 80 men in the POD, yet not one brother offered to share with him.

After the service was over he came over to give me back my Bible. I thought that was it and started to walk away. I heard say, "Hey, man, come here." I didn't know what to think but I came over to where he stood. He reached out and gave me one heck of a bear hug, saying to me, "You are my brother in Christ here." That evening I helped him to fill out an inmate's request form to see the preacher and get his own Bible. A couple of weeks went by, and he hadn't received his own Bible or visit to the jail preacher. On a Thursday evening the guest speaker brought him his Bible. After the meeting was over his name was called—he was being released. He came to me before leaving and gave me one last hug saying in my ear, "Remember—you are my brother in Christ," and he left.

My friend Charlie use to joke around, sometimes too much for being in prison. One evening while we were watching TV he and some of his compadres' were throwing spit wads at each other. I'd often warned him he was going to get killed hitting the wrong person with one. Well, he finally did hit the wrong inmate. He hit one of the biggest brothers in the POD in the eye with one. Charlie was lucky that he was around the TV where there were enough inmates to keep that guy from killing him. Luckily this happened just before the 10 p.m. lock-down. The guy was still fuming. In fact, he came to our cell after we were safely locked away in the cell to warn Charlie he was going to kick his ass the next day. We didn't know it then, but the guy was leaving the next day. I kept telling Charlie he needed to get a message to the guy that night apologizing to him. Charlie was young and wiry, but no match for this guy. The next morning came, and I heard our cell door unlock. We were not safe. As I went to leave to go get breakfast I saw the guy making a bee line for our cell and Charlie. I told Charlie he was coming, and he'd better start talking quick.

Now I'd seen Charlie come close to getting into altercations before, but he was always smart enough not to get into an actual fist fight. The guy got to our cell door, and I was about as afraid of what was about to happen as I'd ever been. I've mentioned before you get solitary confinement for throwing a punch, even in self defense. I could tell Charlie was tensed up, ready to fight. I wasn't sure what I was going to do if the two started fighting. The guy went right up to Charlie, putting his finger right smack in Charlie's face, and said, "Dude—I'm sorry I didn't apologize to you last night, because it bothered me all night, and I'm sure it did you, too." With that said he went and got his things and left the POD.

It was my second night in the joint. There was an old black and white Hitchcock movie on. I already knew I couldn't hear a word of it, but didn't mind so much, as I'd seen the movie enough to know what was going on. A young white boy was sitting next to me. He just keep a-cussing about why would anyone want to watch an old black and white movie. He was even getting on my nerves. I wanted to tell him to go somewhere else if it bothered him that much—but bitching over any and everything is just a part of prison life. This very buff, older inmate evidently had enough. Luckily the nurse had arrived for evening pill call, and I gotten up to get my meds. While I was in line I watched the big black dude walk over and sucker punch that white boy so hard in the ear it sounded like an M-80 firecracker went off. The boy's feet flew up in the air, and he was out cold. The goon squad made it into the POD quickly and got the black dude off before he killed the boy. We never saw that black dude again in the POD. The white boy lost the hearing in his ear for a while, besides suffering a concussion. No medical personnel were called. The guards just put him in his bunk. Turned out the black dude was related to a police officer in a nearby town. (One of his cousins was put into the POD later and told us.) He did go to solitary for a while, but when I was moved to B POD there was that black dude sitting watching TV. I was scared to death every day after I witnessed an inmate hitting another inmate that vicious.

Inmates live for mail—those that get mail. The prison is really strict about how mail goes out and is received. Once an inmate finishes a letter it cannot be sealed before a guard looks through the contents. There are no hard and fast rules about what can go out, but a guard must look through a letter before it is sealed and put into the mail slot of the guard's console. When I first arrived the envelopes were the type one had to lick to seal. At this time the guards would physically look through the contents, upon being satisfied it is okay, would hand it back to the inmate to lick and seal. Later on, the commissary, where inmates had to purchase envelopes at 5 cents apiece, sold envelopes with the tab that you'd peel off to expose the sticky part. Then the guards started sealing the letters as well. The guards never tried to read any of a letter of mine. Incoming mail was already opened. Incoming mail had a good many restrictions. One was that there could not be stamps or envelopes for the inmate to use. Inmates were required to purchase all paper, ink pens, envelopes, and stamps from the commissary, all at an inflated cost. No large packages or boxes were allowed in. Incoming mail was screened before it entered the POD. No type of card with batteries that played songs was allowed. The batteries in them could be used to light cigarettes or other smokeable dope. It was known that drugs like LSD were laced on the lickable envelopes, and there was no way for this to be detected. If there was a way to get something into prison these folks were geniuses. My wife had made me a homemade card, as we didn't have any money. Whoever opened the letter tore off all the little decorations because they had double-sided tape on them. I don't know what that could be used as, but evidently something. No cell wrap was allowed to come into the PODs in letters. This was stupid, as the diabetics' evening sandwiches were wrapped in cell wrap. Mail call was usually at about 2:30 so inmates could read their mail during lock-down before dinner. Mail could also create hostility among inmates. There were those jealous of inmates that got mail all of the time. An inmate might get a "Dear John" letter, making him upset and sometimes hostile. A cell mate might get into his mate's personal letters. Like most everything else in prison, if there was a way to make an inmate mad, they would find it. I wrote my wife over 70 letters while in jail. I felt for inmates who would send out lots of letters to so-called family and friends only to get them returned. I also helped a few inmates to write letters.

TIME

Whenever I think about time, the song, "Time in a Bottle," by the late Jim Croce, comes to mind. Time is the one thing all prisoners have in common. If there was a way to put time in a bottle and sell it, inmates would all be rich.

Almost 24/7 inmates do nothing but think about time. I spent the day wishing time and my life away. While watching TV one thinks about the times sitting on a nice soft couch at home. Maybe sitting watching TV with a loved one beside us. Times with our children sitting or lying in our laps watching TV with us. The shows always have you going back in time to events they are showing, and remembering happy times, sitting while petting one's dog or cat, thinking about all the time you would spend sitting in your favorite recliner relaxing watching TV, maybe even taking a nap.

Lying in those metal bunks brought back the thought of the time one was snuggled up all nice, warm, and comfortable in a bed. The times you woke up to pound your pillow to fluff it up so you'd be more comfortable. There were many times I rolled off my bunk while sleeping.

All the hours in the day that one spends sitting in a plastic lawn chair just thinking about time are pure hell. Every day was a challenge to maintain one's mental state. That is what 80 men in a POD do the majority of their time. Try to figure out how to make the time of day pass faster. What time it is constantly bothers inmates, as there are no clocks anywhere in the POD, and most guards won't tell you. Watches are not permitted for inmates. What can I do today to pass the time? Should I try to sleep the day away? But then I'll be up, miserable, all night long. I'll play cards to pass this day away, remembering that sitting in one place for more than an hour or so hurts your ass so bad. Your ass always hurts from sitting in those damn plastic chairs, passing time.

Time becomes the biggest mental part of being incarcerated. Time can cause a person to lose his mind to the point he no longer wants to live. Time can cause a person to not care what happens to him if he attacks a guard or another inmate. Time makes one go crazy.

God, faith, loved ones, and friends are the only way I survived in prison. Thinking about the time with each of them in the past, present, and future is the only consoling means to maintain one's sanity. I read the Bible a lot. I also got a copy of the 2008 Daily Guidepost, and faithfully read and wrote about my prayers and feelings for that day. My life began to change. Passing time each day was still very painful, but I began to develop methods to get in touch with my faith and love for others. This change in my attitude began to give me a different perspective on dealing with time each new day. I began to not just know God was with me; I could feel him. This new-found faith began to help me with the problem of time.

MY RELEASE

My time to leave finally came when my name was called out to "Bag and bag it!" meaning to get my stuff in your cell packed, as I was leaving. I already talked about what happened when I walked out of the POD for the last time. I walked down the hallway to the out-take room to turn in what belonged to the prison and got the clothes I'd worn upon arriving. I was so excited I was fumbling things, and could hardly get my civilian clothes on quick enough. From there I went to the room where you call to have someone come and get you, then wait. Fortunately my wife was waiting at home for my phone call. She'd already been up at the prison the day before to get me, as my lawyer told her I was being released the day before. The judge delayed his decision for one more day. This time the call was from me, and she was on her way to get for real.

The wait was unbearable, as I was so excited to finally not just see my wife, but to actually hold and kiss her. I spent most of the time waiting praying and thanking the good Lord for getting us through everything and allowing for this time to finally come.

I saw our truck pull into the visitors' parking area, and began to run to her. I had a bag of personal items, like clothes I'd bought, the letters from her, some toiletry items, and the like, but I was just a-running to her. She began to run to me, too. It was just like the embraces you see on TV. We met, hugged, swung in a circle, and kissed. This was the best greeting in my life. We then made our way to the parked truck.

JAIL

It was close to midnight by now, and the moon and stars were out. The prison was a ways out in the country, so I didn't see any neon signs or anything for a while. I did feel a bit queasy from all of the excitement, but also from not being use to movement from the vehicle. The ride seemed long. We finally reached the edge of town, and the neon lights of all the stores were lit up. I wasn't used to colors or the brightness of the lights either.

Everything that was normal to me before now seemed foreign. Colors, the air, smells, and even food. I couldn't eat much of anything spicy for a while, since my taste buds and body had become used to the bland food. My teeth continue to hurt. We went to Wal-Mart to get some supplies, and had to leave, as the smells upset me. I began to realize this returning to a normal life was going to be anything but normal. I was going to have to adjust, and my wife was going to have to put up with something we hadn't expected, my getting used to living in the normal world.

That Sunday was Easter Sunday, and my wife and I went to church together. I held her hand through most of the service. It was wonderful, and I quietly thanked God for being back in his house.

Time has passed. We moved from the bad neighborhood. We now lived in our dream house. Our dogs seemed happier with their new surroundings. (They could see out the back, wrought-iron fencing). A very dear friend helped us get into house. Friends from work put in a lot of hard work and sweat getting us moved. It could not have gone better. Friends came out of the woodwork to help us. It was overwhelming.

Our two dogs enjoyed having more room to romp about, and have gotten use to my taking up my spot in the bed. They are back to sleeping at the foot of the bed now. I am so very blessed that my bosses were able to hold onto my job, and everyone has treated me like I'd just been on an extended vacation. Life is wonderful! God has a plan for everything and everyone.

LOVED ONES

I was going to end my writing with the jailhouse religion, but God knows where he stands in my mind, heart, and soul. I want to say to all those whose prayers, love, kindness, and help in every imaginable way sustained us, how much all you did means to me and to my wife. Without the love, support, and sheer strength from this woman I never would have made through this. I know the Lord understands what I am saying, as she will tell you HE was with her through all of this, too.

When all this started my wife and I thought it was going to be just her and me trying to work through the mess. Then out of the blue family and friends began to support us. It was a learning curve for all of us, as the prison system does everything in its power to make a person in prison live in pure hell. I'd like to tell our judicial system where it can go, but I don't think God would approve.

I have never witnessed so much dedication from so many people. There was the money my family had to pay for a good lawyer, that was necessary to get me out—lots of money. But there were others who sacrificed time away from their families to help my wife out by making sure she had food and she ate it. Folks watched our dogs to help give her a much-needed break and rest. Many helped pack all of our furniture and personal items, load them onto pickup trucks and trailers, unload the stuff, and put it where it went in our new home. We had to move to get away from the drugs and violence. We thoroughly enjoy our new home. And last but not least, my coworkers. I would not have my job right now if not for the goodness and loyalty I received from so many of the folks I work for and with. God bless you all!

SOLUTION

Since submitting my experience in writing for publication I've been stumbling over in my mind that there is something just not right with what I've written. Now I didn't start out writing this book as "Here is the problem, and I have the solution." During the past few years working in the private sector, the good companies no long offer employees to submit or allow personnel to come forward with a problem. If you feel you have a legitimate problem it is very much welcome, but the difference now is—you must bring at least some thought towards a solution to the table also. No more just bitching. By writing my experience I do identify a lot of the problems with our penal system. I even accuse the penal system, and I strongly feel rightfully so, that the majority of problems with prisons in America are due to the mentality and methods they have in place for our incarceration process. I am talking about any correctional detention facility in the USA. I believe what I am about to write would be a small contribution to a partial solution for a part of our penal system that is doable, and would prove beneficial to all.

This is not a new concept. When I was attending college I was the president of the sociology department's student society. I set up tours to prisons from the maximum-security to the minimum-security facilities. It all made sense. I witnessed some of what I'm about to suggest from these tours and other things I've seen or read about. I'll get to the cost later.

What I will do, here, is not go through the stages that some states do. They implement this system of difference stages of security used to bring a very long-term violent offender down through the process in order for them to be released back into society with a sense of belonging.

There are 20,000 inmates that are arrested annually in this county alone. These inmates just sit in the detention facility, for varying time periods, doing absolutely nothing. The report stated that the facility remains full daily, and that more additions are needed. These additions would be a mirror image of the present facilities. All concrete, metal electronic doors and a common area. Working with folks in the construction profession, I know the high cost of such facilities. They try to justify that cost savings to the public. Building these facilities use tons of concrete, metal, electronic surveillance, and take fewer guards for maintaining the security of the facility.

The majority of inmates in a detention facility are there for parole violation of some sort. Most inmates are in the facility awaiting their trial date. Think about this. The offense they committed is not dangerous enough to keep them behind bars, but because they cannot afford the high monthly cost of paying their probation or parole officer, or they miss a scheduled monthly meeting with a probation or parole officer, or they pee dirty for alcohol or usually smoking some marijuana, or they write another bad check because they have no money, or strayed further out of their yard than their probation monitor allows (one was putting his garbage can out to the edge of the road. It slipped over the curb; he had to step into the road to pull it back up and ended up back in the detention center for 90 days for a second offense to probation because he was a couple of feet from what his monitor had been set to extend out from his front door) and lots of other minor violations to the restrictions placed upon them. The majority of first-time offenders are in for a situation involving alcohol, using drugs (not dealing them), writing bad checks, and other minor infractions.

Yet these people end up in a facility designed to be as tough or worse than some of your maximum security federal penitentiaries (Ft. Leavenworth, Fulton County, and even the now-closed Alcatraz).

This is no exaggeration. For any politician, newspaper people, ministers, or concerned citizens, just try to go to your local detention facility. You will not be allowed in to view any of what I am saying first hand. None of you, regardless of your status, power, community influence, or even the right to know and see—you will not be allowed into where the prisoners are kept! And why not? Because the system does not want anyone to know the reality of what is actually taking place in these facilities. The public does not want to know either until one of their loved ones is placed into such a facility.

My recommendation for change sounds simple, and I know most objections would be the cost. My recommendation would be to make a major focus on making the facility fit the crime, and rehabilitation of inmates the major focus to our penal system. What an idiot thought. Detention facilities and time in prison are to punish, to ruin peoples lives, as not just the inmate's life that is ruined such as family and loved ones also. They will never have an opportunity to return to society and contribute in a positive, productive way.

Build more of the minimum-security facilities. These facilities would be designed with structures involving rehabilitation programs instead of mere sitting around for hours, or being locked down most of 24 hours. These prison complexes generally have enough land that is considered necessary for the guards to see an inmate escaping. The rehabilitation would focus on mandatory drug and alcohol programs, anger management, behavioral classes, GED and other educational programs, technical training, and other programs designed to help inmates. In addition there would be jobs in trades for which inmates would receive some sort or certificate for work they'd either learned to do, or had done while incarcerated. Trustees could be selected from the long-term prisons to monitor inmates in these types of facilities. These prisoners selected to be trustees and live at the minimum-security facility would have requirements to meet to even be eligible for selection, requirements such as: they would already have to have served a reasonable amount of their prison sentence. During that time they would have to display a number of documented prerequisites, attending programs such as the drug and alcohol dependence, anger management, and other programs that prisons offer to prisoners on a voluntary basis. Reports from guards would be reviewed to ensure they behaved in a civil manner every day. Bonuses for leadership qualities demonstrated by attending or even organizing prayer groups, helping other inmates in whatever capacity needed, and just demonstrating a good, positive attitude, much like the qualities a parole board should be reviewing to release a prisoner. The trustees job would be hands-on work, not merely additional supervision that the guards provided. Guards would be there to promote good behavior, participation, and a better quality of life for an inmate serving his time.

The housing facility would merely be constructed like a large, wide-open gymnasium. There would be open sleeping quarters. Toilet and shower areas would be private from the standpoint that no one could just look in, but would be constructed for several inmates at a time. The cooking and dining area would also be separated from other areas, much like a high-school dining area.

Open-framed facilities would be constructed for the mandatory programs to attend, and for places where trades of different types would be taught and conducted, such as sewing, wood, and metal working, electronics, and whatever trades were deemed cost effective to offer inmates. The products produced could be for use in the penal system. The sewing classes could be repairing inmates' uniforms. Inmates in wood and metal shops could be fixing items that needing repairing or replacing within the prisons. Same for electronic courses and work. Outdoor farm land could be used to produce food for the prison. There would also be the outdoor recreation for inmates to use. I know none of this is rocket science, and none are some new grandiose idea I have come up with.

So—what about the costs? First and for most, how expensive is it for the present penal system to have a revolving door of inmates? People who serve time are returned to the same environment, with the same attitudes they came to prison with, and nothing is achieved. Actually there is an end product to the present system: a more violent and much scarier society for us all to live in. The day an inmate is released from prison is very often the worst day of his life. Many have no family left, no friends, no money, and no job to return to. What is wrong with providing inmates with an opportunity to improve themselves, to try and make an honest living for a change, to be able to get out and provide for their families instead of drinking, doing drugs, and robbing to survive on their own? Give them a certificate of their achievements to hand to a potential employer. Pat inmates who deserve one on the back, and reward those who truly demonstrate they want to be good, hard-working citizens. I witnessed first hand that the majority of inmates are just that. They really want to get back the family they lost. They want to get back to a hard-working job they lost. They want love and happiness from life just like the rest of us. Think about how many times you might have been one drink away from being in their position. Or the time the police officer cut you slack and didn't arrest you for whatever you were doing that was actually against the law. There are many of you walking around that should be in the Bob Barker flip flops just like those who got caught or didn't get the break you did. Life is very fickle and fragile. Count your blessings if you or a loved one have never experienced any of what I have written. This could be many of you looking from the inside out, if not today then tomorrow.

FOOD FOR THOUGHT

Prisons are designed so that prison officials and especially the guards, enjoy the anonymity and autonomy that protective isolation from all of society behind prison doors and walls afford them. As to the inhumane treatment that takes place there, no one from the outside is allowed in to the actual prison to see what is going on. Local news reporters only see what prison officials allow them to see. They only get to interview prisoners that prison officials allow them to interview. The purpose is to keep the public uninformed as to what actually takes place behind those closed doors.

This penal system reminds me of the old movies we were shown when I was getting my degree in psychology. They were on how mental institutions used to be run. How inhumane those helpless individuals were treated! They were helpless as to what was happening to them at the hands of those in charge of overseeing them, the very people that were supposed to be taking care of them. That is exactly what is taking place in the penal system in American now. The pictures of how inmates were treated at Guantanamo Bay by military prison officials is an exaggeration of what takes place in our prisons, but not by much. The entire focus of the media on was on displaying the nakedness of the prisoners. The reality is that the authorities in running our penal system have the same autonomy and the same protection from exposure as those who ran our mental institutions and the prisons like Guantanamo Bay had. If not for a few people who filmed or took pictures and shared them, the public would continue to be ignorant of the atrocities at Guantanamo Bay. It took exposure before the loud cries of the public created an immediate call for change from the lawmakers of our nation to take any action for the treatment of these prisoners.

There is now some exposure to the facilities of our penal system throughout the nation. It is a show called *Lockup* (I think). I can hardly watch it. From day one of being incarcerated the name of the game in America becomes apparent—to maintain one's mental abilities. Watch this show and others shows like it if you dare.

There are plenty of web sites, like www.bobbarkerprisons.com, one can search to see pictures and read stories that are true about prison life. One other thing. When you watch TV shows like COPS, watch to see the unnecessary use of excessive force, the violent brutality used often by the police, and how the police are aware of where the cameras are and often take people out of sight where it obvious more than just handcuffing a person is taking place.

There was a study conducted by then former Mayor of San Antonio, Texas, Henry Cisneros, on police and crime. He took the police out of the so-called ghettos of the city and placed them in the middle- to upper-class neighborhoods of the city. The results were, the crimes weren't where the people were; the crimes were where the police were focusing their surveillance on. The police made just as many arrests in the more affluent areas of San Antonio as they had been making in the lower-class neighborhoods. I believe there were some differences in what the arrests were over. For example, instead of making busts for methamphetamines in the ghettos, the busts were for crack cocaine in the affluent neighborhoods. The violent crimes in the ghettos sounded much more horrendous then in affluent neighborhoods.

If a killer uses a knife to stab someone multiple times, that just sounds so horrific compared to a person being shot and killed. Old bicycles and old cars are stolen in the ghettos. Top-of-the-line motorcycles, BMWs, and Corvettes are stolen in the higher-class neighborhoods. The point is that violence in both areas is just as abundant. It is just that the methods, weapons, and items stolen are different in the different neighborhoods. Then there are the appearances and noises made by police. In the upper-class neighborhoods the sight of police cars driving up and down their roads is frowned upon. The populace is much more tolerant of that helicopter flying over property to detect heat given off from pot-growing houses or buildings or drug-making chemical labs in the ghettos than in the affluent neighborhoods. How many ghetto homes or building have things like tanning beds, saunas and hot tubs, or real green houses in or on their property? Besides, who is going to get the police department's attention with complaints about the very loud noises of helicopters flying over their homes while they are trying to sleep at night?

I've been reading in the news about funding for public defenders. There is a murder trial taking place in Georgia that is using up all the money the state legislature put into the annual public defender's funds. Now there is another murder, and the defense is complaining the media, and very loudly, that they do not have the money to properly put a defense together for the accused. The public-defender's office cannot hire the proper personnel to do the legal research, investigation, and they have not been paid to date for months of work these public defenders have already put into the defending the accused. Now where does this leave the thousands of other indigent people arrested who need a Public Defender that is willing to put forth the type of defense that as lawyers then have sworn an oath to uphold? Justice in America has become a joke. The Georgia solution is to get rid of the cost of the public defenders office all together. This puts indigent prisoners back in the hands of young, unskilled, and inexperienced trial lawyers.

CONCLUSION

Now I don't think our entire judicial system is totally evil, but there are definitely areas where we have people and laws in place that are just plain inhumane. Changes are drastically needed so people's lives are not totally destroyed by a legal system that has been recognized in the past as a model for the rest of the world to follow. We are far from being any such model now. I pray things can get changed around in today's society so that our judicial system can get back to doing what is right and eliminating the wrongs. This includes more than just the lawyers, judges, and others deemed directly associated with what goes on in our prisons and courts. Society in general has turned its back on what is right and wrong in our judicial system. Most of what the citizens see are the tax dollars being spent on building these prisons, and how full their local prisons are. No one seems to be asking just exactly who are the people we are filling our prisons with?

I've pointed out before that your local police know exactly where the crime and violence is located in your communities. The police even know the names of the criminals, gang members, and crooks and where they live. So why don't they go arrest them? One reason is your prisons are full of a casual pot smoker, a petty thief, a one-time shoplifter, and so on. Probation Violation is the primary reason for our prisons being over filled. Are these the type of people we are spending millions of our tax dollars to see put behind bars? There isn't the room to keep the long-term hardened criminals. The attitude seems to be, it is easier to just let them take care of themselves by killing each other. Also the police want to know where the hard-core criminals are located so they can keep the other areas of a city clean. If the criminals started spreading out all over a city the police would lose total control on crime. The point is our society needs to take a good, hard look at what is taking place with our judicial system to make sure it is what we really want. People watch TV shows and say, "That will never happen to me or my family," or "That is so bizarre the odds are so far reaching it will never happen to me." You probably don't have to look much further than what is going on in your own neighborhood to find out these police accounts are true. Ever think your mail has been stolen? Gotten a letter from a credit agency that you didn't know you were behind in bills? Better watch your mail. The news tells how poorly the police are being paid across the nation. This is a major problem. How can cities attract the best possible police force if they don't pay them? These men and women do put their lives on the line. The other side to this is that they are also tempted to cross the line to better provide for their families.

Then there is the question, "Just what is it our judicial systems, prisons in particular, are doing to improve society?" I have seen TV shows where prisons have programs to help inmates find a trade for them to be able to find work once they are released or to be a productive part of society even though they will be in prison for a long time. This place I was in offered nothing. It was a place for one to sit and go mentally ill or get even madder at society. This is nothing but a place for inmates to build a lot of hate for everything, and everyone.

There were the few selected to go to work details, but most of these jobs were nothing more than free slave labor for the prison. Most inmates have nothing to look forward to once it is time for them to leave: no family or friends, no job to return to, nothing else but to go right back to the only life they know, drugs, violence, and self preservation! Any means possible to survive. The problem inmates face here is that the judicial system is evidently satisfied with way things operate. Spend more taxpayers' money on building more prisons, and keeping the prisons full.

Like they say, "There are two sides to every story." I have provided my side, my perspectives, and my views about my personal experience of being incarcerated. My lawyer can probably tell about all the behind-the-scenes negotiations that took place that I am unaware of to get me out. How, his educational background and his local reputation are a major part of what my family paid for. The same is probably true about guards and police, how they have to deal with each arrestee or inmate as if he were dangerous. To try to treat each arrestee or inmate as an individual is an impossible task. Their jobs might not appear important, but society has set up the process, and they are merely following the laws and rules as they are instructed. This all points to a judicial system that has no concern when it comes to rights or rehabilitation of prisoners. There are very few prisons set up for any type of rehabilitation. Guilt or innocence appears to be based upon who you know, how much money you have to defend yourself, and how under crowded or overcrowded the prison is. Again, I'm not saying a prison should be a resort for prisoners. All I am saying is that the fairness of right and wrong needs to be put back into the equation. If there are other perspectives on what I have written, then don't sit there getting mad—write a book!

TV news rescently showed the place I was incarcerated holds almost 600 inmates and is full to capacity year 'round. In fact, this county often transports inmates to other counties if room is available at them or puts 3 inmates into a room with 2 bunks. One will have to sleep on the floor. The proposed solution by the local politicians is to add new facilities. Why not look at the actual numbers, who is constantly being arrested, and are these arrests necessary? Instead they should be looking at the system.

This brings me back to parole violators. They are not in the prison because of the act they committed. That act wasn't bad enough to keep them in prison. They are continually brought back because most cannot meet the conditions of their probation—*money*! How in the world can a person who gets a laundry list of arrests for probation or parole violation get a job? Not a job just to live on, but to pay fees to their probation officer of up to $150 monthly. They can't. So when the probation officer gets tired of not getting his money from one of his clients, he calls the police to have him picked up. I never knew that those let out on probation or parole paid money to the probation officer, let alone in amounts this high. And who determines what a probation officer receives monthly? The range can be from somewhere around $50 a month to $150. There is no correlation between the amount paid and the crime committed. It depends on how much money you could afford to get a hired lawyer. Those using public defenders usually end up paying the most.

Why doesn't the news have at least one major drug bust to report each and every night? I've already answered that question, but with this new information I obtained it is worth repeating. There is no room in the detention facilities or prisons to bring in a large number of arrestees. Also a major drug bust would begin to cost money. After an inmate has been in the facility so long he turns from being a profit to costing the penal system large amounts of money. Busting the dealers becomes a long-term process, requiring true legal defenses, and is a lose-lose situation for the judicial system. As I said, the police are satisfied with knowing who and where the major drugs are in their jurisdiction. As long as these criminals do not tend to stray beyond their territories then the police leave them alone. The police will actually, in a sense, defend and protect what is taking place in their jurisdiction. Unless these individual drug users or dealers get out of control all is well.

Why are these prisons, jails, or whatever you want to call them are so over-crowded? The penal system is a major part of the finances of the city, county, state, and federal governments. Evidently a very profitable one, if the solution is to build brand new facilities. And why should politicians and the public care about who is being arrested? They have the numbers to justify the new build-ings. That is all the taxpayers are concerned about. Will the judicial system fill the new facilities is what satisfies the taxpayers concerns over the money spent. And who can blame anyone for this mind set? Like most everyone else, I've always been concerned with the economy, raising a family, and what is going on at work. Why should the average Joe care about what is taking place in the penal system as long as reports show us society is well and good?

The penal system plays a major role in local politics. Politicians don't care about how prisoners are treated; they just want prisons full of prisoners.

I'd also like to see a report on the after effects from being tazered. Every joint in my body aches, and it gets worse daily. I can barely lift my arms above my shoulder for the pain. My neck hurts to turn. The joints in my hip, knee, and feet ache when I walk. But the worst is my hands. When I wake up both are always really sore. It takes me a while just to be able to open my fingers. As the day goes on some of the joints begin to loosen up, but I can't sit for very long. Just typing this book is painful.

I'm also experiencing problems with my organs—things like going to the bathroom. At first I just passed it off as being the change from my digestive tract being use to the prison food. It is more. My kidneys are not functioning right. I don't go for two, three, or even four days at a time. My kidneys and other diges-tive organs always feel bloated and ache. I'm sure some of this is due to old age. But now taking not even a spoonful of fiber in my morning coffee has helped. I now wonder if being tazered has taken its toll on my internal organs as well.

Then there is my blood pressure. After my spending such a long period of time not being given my proper medicine, my doctor and I have been experimenting with new and different blood-pressure medicine. I still experience dizziness, tiredness, and an internal jitteriness that is new and very strange to me. Being tazered and the not being provided my proper medicine I'm sure took its toll on my heart.

The body was not meant to be electrocuted, and that is what being tazered is. Doctors need to look into the effects being tazered has on the body, both short term and long term. Just how detrimental to the body is getting electrocuted? Not all officers carry legal tazers. I don't believe the local sheriff's office provides the brass-knuckle style tazer used on me. In my opinion these were illegal weapons being used on me. Are records keep by police department on the issuing and using of these weapons? Is there a national data base being kept about police and tazers?

Getting back to work was also not as easy as one might think. It took a few weeks for me to get over sounds, smells, driving, and just getting readjusted to what we take for granted as a normal, everyday environment. I'm doing much better. If it hadn't been for the good people I work for and fellow workers I would be another wandering soul on this earth. God has really blessed me that I even have a job and my wife to return to, as I know so many inmates have neither to return to. How scary that must be! All they have to return to is the lifestyle and people that helped to get them into the prison in the first place.

The point to this chapter in my life is that if it hadn't been for God and a lot of loving people I would not have made it through this life's experience. I don't carry any hatred towards anyone involved in this entire event. My writing this book was not to get even with anyone or purposefully get back at anyone. I give thanks during the day, at night, and the morning for what the Lord has blessed me with. I especially thank the Lord for my wonderful wife. Her health is finally returning, and she is more the beautiful, fun-loving person I married. Praise the Lord!

www.ingramcontent.com/pod-product-compliance
Lightning Source LLC
Chambersburg PA
CBHW072204280526
45788CB00002B/871